PATTERNS
from Finished Clothes

PATTERNS
from Finished
Clothes

RE-CREATING THE CLOTHES YOU LOVE

Tracy Doyle

Sterling Publishing Co., Inc.   New York
A STERLING/LARK BOOK

To my husband, without whose help and support I never could have written this book.
Thanks to babysitters and friends, my children afforded me the time to complete it.

Editor: Carol Parks
Art Director: Kathleen Holmes
Photography: Evan Bracken, Light Reflections
Production: Elaine Thompson
Illustrations: Kay Holmes Stafford
Editorial assistance: Mary K. Cooney, Laura Dover

Library of Congress Cataloging-in-Publication Data
Available

10 9 8 7 6 5 4 3 2 1

A Sterling/Lark Book

Published in 1996 by Sterling Publishing Co., Inc.
 387 Park Avenue South, New York, NY 10016

Created and produced by Altamont Press, Inc.
 50 College Street, Asheville, NC 28801

© 1996 by Tracy Doyle

Distributed in Canada by Sterling Publishing, c/o Canadian Manda Group,
 One Atlantic Ave., Suite 105, Toronto, Ontario M6K 3E7

Distributed in Great Britain and Europe by Cassell PLC,
 Wellington House, 125 Strand, London WC2R 0BB, England

Distributed in Australia by Capricorn Link (Australia) Pty Ltd.
 P.O. Box 6651, Baulkham Hills Business Centre, NSW 2153, Australia

ISBN 0-8069-4874-4

CONTENTS

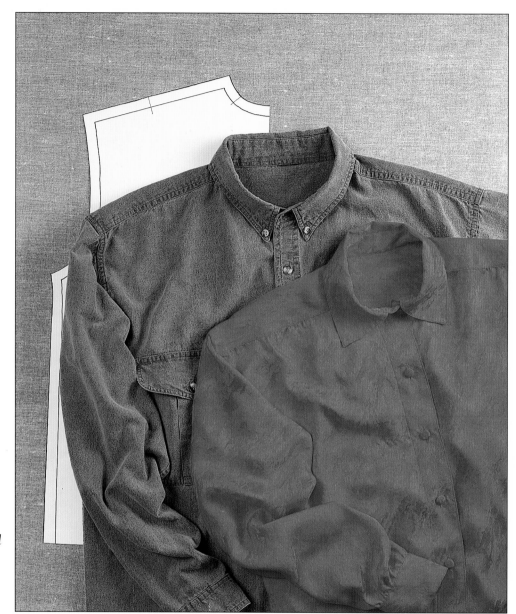

The pattern made from a favorite old denim shirt takes on a sophisticated air when it is sewn up in jacquard-patterned silk. Although the silk and denim fabrics are very different in appearance, both are soft and lightweight, well suited to the shirt's classic lines. The silk was preshrunk to make the new shirt almost as easy to care for as its denim predecessor.

The dressier silk fabric called for change of several style details. To show off the fabric's beautiful drape, the front and lower back were widened by 3/4" (2 cm) at each side to allow slight shirring at the front shoulder and back yoke seamlines. Edgestitching finishes the collar, yoke, front band, and cuffs, replacing the sportier double topstitching on the denim shirt. Omission of the patch pockets also contributes to the dressier look of the new shirt.

Opposite:
With a variety of fabrics and a little imagination, you can create an almost unlimited range of garments from a single pattern. The white shirt at the top—our model on the following pages—provided the pattern for two distinctive copies below it. On the color-blocked shirt, the back was cut slightly longer and a hidden button placket added along the front. Two floral prints fabrics combine for a more subdued shirt, with white piping to highlight the yoke seam.

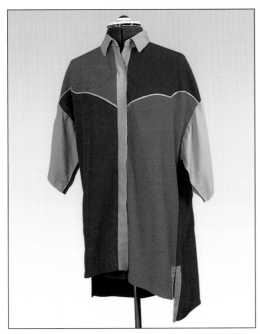

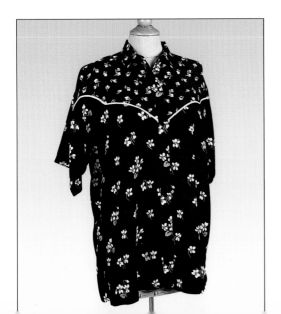

INTRODUCTION

FOR THE OVERWHELMING MAJORITY of sewers, the greatest challenge and the greatest frustration of garment-making is achieving good fit. Most of us have at least a few jackets or pants, expertly made in beautiful fabric, that hang in the back of the closet because they just don't fit as we had hoped. This happens occasionally to even the most experienced sewers, and even when a pattern has been carefully adjusted beforehand.

The solution? Start with a finished garment instead of the pattern. Choose a favorite, one with a flattering style and fit. Make a pattern from it, and you can be confident that your new garment will fit well *before* you invest a fortune in fabric and hours of your precious time.

It is not the least bit difficult to make a pattern from an existing garment! You need no experience in traditional pattern-drafting methods, and you need only a few inexpensive tools. You do not have to take the garment apart in order to copy it. Best of all, the garment made from your new pattern will fit beautifully, and the pattern will cost you next to nothing! It takes less time and is far more rewarding to make a pattern than to start with an expensive commercial pattern, make the alterations, sew the garment, and *then* find that the style doesn't suit you or the fit is unsatisfactory.

Making your own pattern from a ready-made garment will revolutionize your sewing results. When you copy a manufactured garment, you have the benefit of the garment industry's vast experience and talent, and will pick up dozens of valuable tips for efficient construction methods. Careful examination of a manufactured garment can show you innovative ways of approaching construction steps that you have handled in the same old way since you first learned to sew. In addition, you take advantage of the expertise of highly paid designers, and incorporate their styling details into your own garments.

This book was developed to satisfy the pleas of my students for a source of more extensive information on making patterns from ready-to-wear quickly and accurately. The traditional patternmaking process of drafting or draping is too time-consuming and involved for most of us. Our sewing time is limited. We want to be reasonably certain that our efforts will produce clothes that look—and fit—just as we want them to.

If you have sewn enough to be comfortable with basic garment construction methods, you will find patternmaking a breeze. But because some of the procedures and terms probably will be new to you, please take time to read through the section on Basic Copying Techniques before you begin. Your first copy just might be your greatest sewing success!

GETTING SET UP

USE A GOOD-SIZED TABLE for your patternmaking project, preferably in a spot where you can leave your work undisturbed if you have to leave the project unfinished for a time. Make sure the table height is comfortable for you; working on the floor or at a table that is too low can give you a backache.

CORK

You will need a sheet of cork, 3 to 4 feet (1 to 1.2 m) long, 30 inches (76 cm) wide, and 1/8-inch (.5 cm) thick. Cork sheeting is sold in most hardware stores by the foot or in pre-cut lengths. It is light in weight and can be rolled up for storage when not in use. A large cork bulletin board can be substituted if you like.

PLYWOOD

A sheet of plywood is essential for copying a garment that has elastic at the waist, cuffs, or elsewhere. The elastic must be stretched smoothly when you copy the garment, and pins pushed into a cork surface will not hold the stretched elastic firmly enough. With a plywood sheet, pushpins can actually be hammered into the surface to keep the garment securely in place. A sheet of plywood, covered with fabric to prevent snagging a delicate garment, will work for most other copying projects as well.

EQUIPMENT AND TOOLS

Patternmaking requires very few tools. That is one of the great advantages of making your own patterns—the investment in materials is minimal compared to the cost of commercial patterns. Once you have the tools, all you need to make a new pattern is the paper… and a little time!

The tools for copying a garment, clockwise from top: cork sheeting, see-through ruler, paper, paper shears, paper first aid tape, straight pins, fabric marking pen, ballpoint pen, pencil, pushpins, needle-point tracer, smooth tracing wheel.

NEEDLE-POINT TRACER

This specialized tool is used in the fashion and garment industries. It resembles a standard tracing wheel, but it has needle-like spikes that will penetrate the fabric layers and perforate the paper underneath. It is as if a pin were pushed through the garment and into the paper. This wheel works well on all but the most delicate fabrics. Marks left by the tool can be erased by simply rubbing along the perforation line; the fibers will fall back into place.

As an alternative, a sharp, firm pin such as a quilter's pin or pushpin can be used for copying. Push it through the garment seamline at regular intervals to mark the paper beneath.

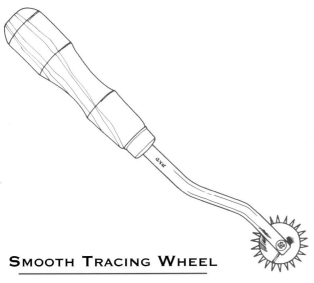

SMOOTH TRACING WHEEL

It is best to use a smooth wheel for fragile fabrics, such as lightweight silk, that might be snagged by the needle-point tracer. This tool works nicely as long as the fabric is fairly thin. Apply pressure as you roll the wheel along the seamline to leave a visible line on the paper below. If the lines are not clear enough to follow, you can place a piece of dressmaker's carbon under the garment as you trace the seams.

When the smooth wheel is used, cork, not plywood, should be used on the work table. The cork's softer surface makes it easier to produce a visible line on the pattern paper.

FABRIC PINS

Straight pins, preferably with glass or plastic heads, are used to secure the garment to the tracing surface. They can also be used in lieu of the methods listed below to mark the garment. Pins are especially helpful when you are working on prints, where other markings might be hard to see.

CHALK OR FABRIC MARKING PENS

Chalk markers or marking pens with water-erasable or disappearing ink can be used in place of pins to mark the garment. These tools may be handier to use than pins; be sure, however, to test them in an inconspicuous spot to make certain the marks can be removed from your garment fabric.

PUSHPINS

Sturdier than straight pins, pushpins are helpful in securing garments that have elastic at the waist, wrists, or lower edge.

CLEAR RULER

You will need a clear ruler with lines at 1/8-inch (.5 cm) intervals for marking seam allowances of varying widths. You do not need a curved ruler because you will be following the curves and the lines of your garment.

TAPE

Either clear or masking tape will work, as long as you can write on it. Paper first aid tape, available at most drugstores, works especially well because it is easy to remove and will not crumple if touched by a hot iron.

SCISSORS

For cutting paper, use an old pair. Paper will dull the blades of your good fabric shears!

PENCILS AND PENS WITH COLORED INK

Ballpoint pens with smudgeproof ink work well. Felt-tip pens aren't recommended because they leave wide lines that will blur if they get wet.

PATTERN PAPER

Many kinds of paper are suitable for patternmaking, with some more durable than others. Regardless of the paper you use, your pattern will last a long time if you follow the suggestions given on page 24.

BUTCHER'S WRAP is one of the more durable papers available, and it has an almost waxy surface. It is only 18 inches (45.5 cm) wide, but since you will be working with just half a garment this width usually will be sufficient. You can always tape on an extension if necessary.

BROWN KRAFT PAPER is inexpensive and can be bought in a roll 30 inches (76 cm) wide.

NEWSPRINT ROLL ends often can purchased at very low cost from the companies that print your local newspapers. You may need to reserve them because printing companies do recycle them. The rolls are approximately 24 inches to 27-1/2 inches (61 to 70 cm) wide and will vary in length.

PATTERN PAPERS are stocked at most fabric and notions stores. Several varieties are available, including nonwoven material printed with a 1-inch (2.5 cm) grid and unprinted tracing tissue. Inexpensive paper in rolls of varying widths can be purchased at art supply and school supply stores.

Whatever kind of paper you choose, there are a few procedures that will help extend the life of your pattern. These are described on page 24.

IN ORDER TO MAKE a successful pattern from your chosen garment, you will want to first study the garment thoroughly. Note the materials and construction techniques used to make it. Remember that your custom pattern won't come with fabric suggestions or sewing instructions; this information will come from the garment itself.

MAKING A FACE SHEET

Each pattern you make should have an accompanying "face sheet." It will contain all of the key information concerning your pattern. At the top of the face sheet, write the name of your garment. It can be a style description, a brand name, or whatever will help you remember the garment. Then make a sketch to help you identify the pattern at a glance. As you analyze the garment, you will want to list the pattern pieces and note your observations about each one. Later you can add fabric yardage requirements, and perhaps attach a swatch each time you use the pattern.

ANALYZING YOUR GARMENT

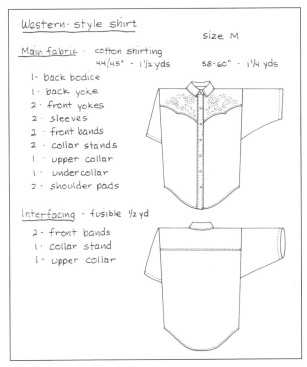

Record pertinent information about each pattern on a face sheet.

GARMENT CONSTRUCTION

Begin your garment analysis with a careful look at the way the garment is made, both inside and out. Observe the kinds of seams and width of the seam allowances used. Was the garment sewn or finished with a serger? Will you use a serger for your new garment, or will you adapt the seam allowances for a standard sewing machine?

Notice how the garment is hemmed. Is the hem single or double? Is it blind hemmed or topstitched? Look at the stitching details. Is there decorative topstitching?

Your study of the original garment will tell you how to construct the new one. If you are copying this particular garment because of its great fit, but see that it was not as well made as it might be, you can use your experience to make your copy a better garment. For manufacturers, speed is essential and shortcuts are often taken in the construction process. Make note of those areas of construction in which you could improve on the workmanship. It is easy, for example, to add a more generous hem or a wider facing.

Make note of any irregularities, such as a piece that is badly sewn or cut slightly off grain. This information can tell you, for example, to copy the left front instead of the right front section.

THE GARMENT COMPONENTS

After taking note of the construction details, make a list on the face sheet of the garment pieces. Note how many of each piece you will have to cut. Group them according to the kind of fabric from which they will be cut.

"Main fabric" (or "self," in the garment industry vernacular) is the fabric from which the largest percentage of the garment is made. "Contrast" is any other fabric used on the outside of the garment. If there is more than one contrast, then label each of them as contrast 1, contrast 2, and so forth. "Lining" is the inner shell of a garment, and sometimes the inner pocket fabric. More than one kind of lining fabric may be used, too. For "interfacing," note whether it is fusible or sew-in, woven or non-woven.

The Garment Fabric

Note the characteristics of the fabric and how they work with the garment design. Is the fabric soft, with considerable drape? Or is it firmly woven and crisp? To ensure the success of your new garment, choose a fabric that is similar in weight, drape, fiber content, and "hand," or feel, to your original. The fit and drape of your garment will directly reflect your fabric choice. A knit fabric, for example, usually is a poor choice for duplication of a garment made of woven fabric.

Be cautious, too, with stripes and geometric patterns unless the original garment features them. Some garment designs simply cannot accommodate such patterns. If you find this is the case with your pattern, make a note on the face sheet.

Manufacturers save money with fabrics, particularly interfacings. You can upgrade the quality of your garment with little extra expenditure and produce a garment that is even better than the original. With interfacings, especially, use the best you can find. It will make little difference to the total cost of your project. Bargain interfacing that shrinks or shreds the first time the garment is washed can ruin an otherwise perfect project.

Do experiment, though. Even the most successful designers sometimes produce less-than-successful garments that never reach the stores. But if you want to make your new garment of a fabric that is very different from the original, buy an inexpensive lookalike fabric and quickly make up your pattern to see whether the new fabric will work. You will save a lot of time and money in the long run.

Always preshrink your fabrics, interfacings included, if you plan to wash the garment. Wash and dry fabrics as you intend to wash your new garment, then press them along the lengthwise grain. For fusible interfacings, dip in warm water for a few minutes, pat out excess water with a towel, and smooth over a rod to dry. Most likely the garment you are copying is well broken in. Even if you make a perfect pattern, your garment will not be perfect if it shrinks a size the first time it is washed.

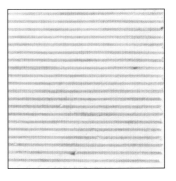

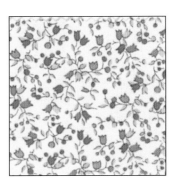

FABRIC GRAIN

Make careful note of the fabric grainline of each garment piece. Was the piece cut on the lengthwise grain, on the crossgrain, or on the bias? If any piece was cut a bit off grain, record that fact on the face sheet, too.

You are probably an experienced sewer, and no doubt have a healthy respect for fabric grainlines. Because fabric grain is so important to the success of your project, please take a minute to review some basic information.

All woven fabric is created by interlacing yarns or threads lengthwise and crosswise at right angles to each other. The direction of these yarns is referred to as the "grain." There are three grainlines to a fabric.

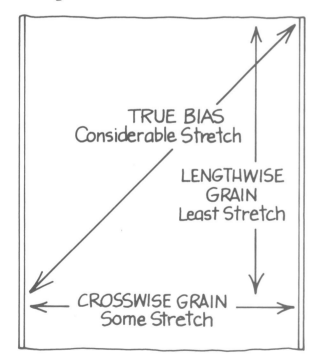

On the lengthwise grain of the fabric, the yarns run vertically, parallel to the finished edges, or selvages. These are the warp yarns. The fabric has greater strength and stability along this grain. Garments are nearly always cut with the lengthwise grain running the length of the body. This affects the drape or hang of the garment when it is worn. Waistbands are one exception to the rule: We need the stability of the lengthwise grain encircling the body.

Crossgrain yarns run from one selvage to the other, across the width of the fabric and at right angles to the lengthwise grain. These threads are the weft, or filler yarns. There is less stability in this direction, with some stretch or give. Knitted fabrics have a great deal more crossgrain stretch than do woven fabrics. Garments are cut with the crossgrain of the fabric across or around the body. Once again, there will be occasional and intentional deviations from this rule—for example, the yoke of a striped shirt will often be cut on the lengthwise fabric grain to add visual interest.

True bias runs diagonally across the fabric at a 45-degree angle to the lengthwise and crosswise grains. The fabric has the most stretch along the bias.

If you wish to change the grainline on a pattern, be aware that the resulting garment may be very different in appearance and fit. You can take artistic license with grainlines, but you may have to pay a price.

NOW IS THE TIME to try on the garment and critique the fit. If you weren't satisfied with the general fit of the garment, you probably wouldn't be copying it in the first place. Let's say, however, that you love the style of the garment, but you have perhaps changed a size since you bought it. Here are a few tips for dealing with some common problem areas.

Put the garment on and look at it carefully. On the face sheet, next to the listing for the appropriate pattern piece, note any changes you will need to make.

CHANGING THE FIT

Suppose a skirt or a pair of pants is a bit tight around the tummy or hips. Measure down from the waist to where the problem area begins and estimate the necessary increase in width at that point. Make a notation on the face sheet to add from that point downward. It is a good idea to cut the pattern with extra seam allowance for the entire seam to allow for further adjustment as you sew.

Now try this trick: Once the fit has been adjusted and fine tuned on the new garment, neatly trim away the extra seam allowance from the garment. Realign the trimmed piece on the pattern. Now trim that same amount from the pattern. The next time you use the pattern, you will have a perfect fit with no further adjustments needed.

If the fit adjustment extends to the waist, then the adjoining waistband will also need to be lengthened. Remember that when you adjust a pattern piece, the same amount of change must be made on any adjoining pattern pieces as well.

ALTERATIONS AND ADJUSTMENTS

CHANGING THE LENGTH

When you lengthen a skirt or dress, it is a good idea to add a little extra to your estimate, as it is hard to tell exactly how the garment will look when it is finished. The excess fabric can always be trimmed off later, and the pattern adjusted accordingly.

Suppose your skirt is cut on the bias and the hem now hangs unevenly. This is a common complaint. You can avoid duplicating the flaw by straightening the hem on the original garment before making the copy. Put the skirt on and have a friend mark an even hemline, measuring up from the floor with a yardstick or hem marker. On your pattern, add hem allowance below the marked line.

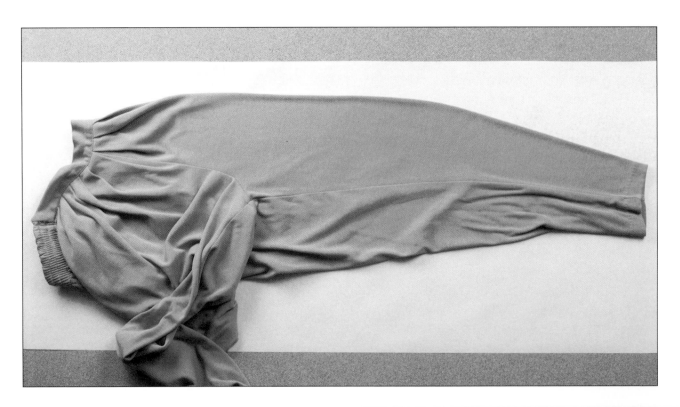

OUT-OF-SHAPE GARMENTS

Another problem worth mentioning often occurs with knits and other garments made of very soft fabrics. Knit pants are famous for developing "knees." They seem to take on a life of their own, looking as if you were still in them, as if they could almost get up and walk away!

This excess fabric will have to be pinched out when you make your copy. Follow the directions for copying pants, page 81, to the point where you have folded the leg down the center. Then fold out a pie-shaped piece of fabric so the leg will lie along the straight grain line, as shown.

Elbows in knits and loosely woven fabrics can create the same problem. They can be dealt with in the same way.

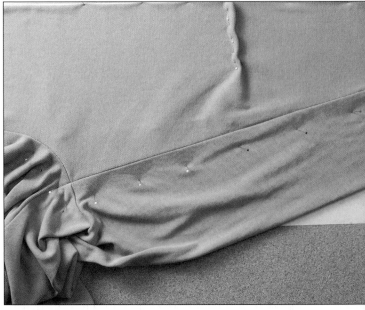

Any other misshapen areas of fabric should be patted into shape before the garment is copied. Observe the fabric grainlines and adhere to them strictly when you make the pattern.

THERE ARE NONE! At first, the prospect of assembling a garment without an instruction sheet to guide you may seem a bit overwhelming, but all you need to do is find a starting point and build on it. The experience may free you forever from commercial pattern directions. If you have been sewing for a while—and you probably have if you are attempting a patternmaking project—you've most likely reached the point where you simply glance over the instruction sheet for helpful tips, then make the garment in your own way.

LOOK AT THE GARMENT FOR CONSTRUCTION TIPS

Let the garment show you the construction sequence as you study the seams. It is easy to see, for example, that the sleeve was set in before the side seams were sewn, and so on. As a rule of thumb, a garment is best sewn together by working as far as possible with flat pieces. By the time you have made your pattern you will be so familiar with your garment that it will go together with no trouble at all. Remember, you can always refer to your original garment for guidance.

If a particular construction detail causes bewilderment, pull out one of your old commercial patterns with a similar feature or look up the technique in a good basic sewing book.

SEWING INSTRUCTIONS

A careful study of ready-to-wear construction will teach you dozens of timesaving tips. For instance, in preparing to copy a lined jacket you will have to remove one of the shoulder pads. How can you reach it? When you examine the jacket to find access to the pad, you may find that several inches along one of the sleeve lining seams have been topstitched closed. That part of the seam was originally left open to allow the seamstress access for finishing, then it was stitched from the outside after the jacket was turned right side out through the opening. The seam is out of view inside the sleeve. You can open just this short section of the seam to remove the pad.

The ready-to-wear industry has many wonderful secrets just waiting to be discovered. Take time to shop the designer departments of good stores just to study details of styling and construction. You will pick up many valuable tips that can be put to good use in your future sewing projects.

FABRIC REQUIREMENTS

The best way to determine the amount of fabric you will need for a garment is to lay out the pattern pieces on a folding cardboard cutting mat, the kind printed with a 1-inch (2.5 cm) grid, or on a large mat made for use with a rotary cutter.

If all the pieces will be cut from doubled fabric, mark a line on the mat to represent half the fabric width. Designate one edge of the marked area as the fabric fold and the other as the selvages. Lay out the pattern pieces in the marked area. Pay careful attention to the grainlines, and allow a little leeway at the selvage edges.

If you don't have a mat, substitute large sheets of paper taped together as necessary. Make the sheet at least 2 yards (2 m) long, longer if your work surface can accommodate it. Draw lines 18, 22, 27, and 30 inches (46, 56, 69, 76, and 81 cm) from one edge and parallel to it to represent doubled fabric 36, 44, 54, and 60 inches (90, 112, 138, 152, and 162 cm) wide respectively. If you sew with the wider knitted fabrics, add a line at 32 inches (81 cm) as well.

Lay out the pattern pieces as instructed above. With each piece, measure from each end of the marked grainline to the edge or line on the paper to ensure the pieces are placed correctly with respect to fabric grain.

It is a good idea to do the pattern layout for several different fabric widths. Note yardage requirements on the pattern face sheet and you will have a ready reference for your next trip to the fabric store.

SOME OF THESE CONCEPTS and definitions may be familiar to you. Others are used primarily in the patternmaking and garment industries and may be new even to experienced sewers. Take a few minutes to read through them before your begin your patternmaking project.

SEAM ALLOWANCE

Commercial pattern manufacturers nearly always use 5/8 inch (1.5 cm) as a standard seam allowance. In the garment industry the standard is 1/2 inch (1.3 cm) for most seams, with 1/4 inch (.7 cm) for collars, front bands, and facings. For your own patterns, you should use the seam allowance with which you are most comfortable working. You can make your own rules. Keep in mind, though, that a 5/8-inch (1.5 cm) seam allowance may add unwanted bulk to the garment and will often have to be trimmed after the seam is sewn. For that reason, industry standards will be used in the patternmaking instructions since those are what you are likely to see in the garment you are copying. Whatever seam allowance you use, be sure to note on each pattern piece the amount of seam allowance included.

Commercially made garments are often sewn with a machine that produces a chain-stitched seam and overcast edge at the same time. The machine is similar to the five-thread overlock available to home sewers, but it produces a slightly wider trimmed seam allowance. When you make your pattern, you will need to adjust the seam allowances for the equipment and construction process you plan to use.

PATTERNMAKING TERMS

SQUARING OFF A SEAM

It will be necessary to make perfect right angles at some points where the edge of the pattern piece meets a fold or an adjacent edge. Use the lines of a clear ruler to line up the correct seam allowance at a right angle for the first 1/2 inch (1.5 cm) or so. Then continue the line, following the contour of the garment. A small carpenter's square also works well for this task.

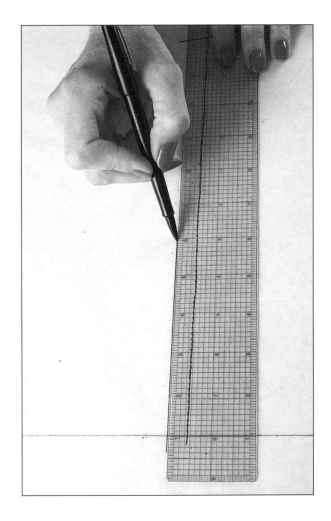

WALKING THE PATTERN

No, you won't need a leash for this procedure. This patternmaking term describes the simulation of sewing two garment pieces together. Place two adjacent pattern pieces with their seamlines one on top of the other, aligned at an edge. Then, with the point of a pencil, "walk" one pattern piece to the other along the stitching line to assure they will fit together correctly when sewn.

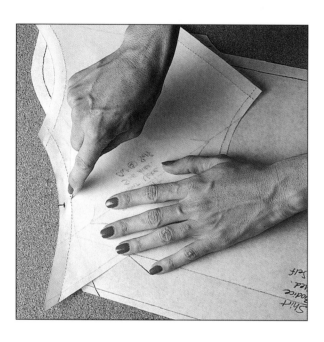

NOTCHES

Commercial patterns have a series of single and double triangles that designate matching points on seamlines. These are called "pimple notches." It is somewhat awkward to cut those little triangles, and they are not very precise as guides for matching. A series of small clips into the seam allowance is much more accurate. Use one to designate matching points on front pieces, and two for back pieces. Take care to make your clips no more than 1/4 inch (.5 cm) deep on a standard seam allowance. You will still need to use pimple notches on 1/4-inch (.7 cm) seam allowances since the width won't permit decent-sized clips.

THE DITCH

When two pieces of fabric are sewn with right sides together, the seamline on the right side is referred to as the "ditch." The instruction to "stitch in the ditch" is often given for attaching a waistband and the like.

SHAPED SEAM ALLOWANCE

The seam allowances on garment hems, cuffs, and other points at which fabric is folded back should be shaped. Perhaps you have tried at some time to shorten a pair of tapered pants and found that the circumference of the lower edge of the leg was smaller than that of the leg at the point where the hem was to be stitched in place. A shaped seam allowance would have prevented the problem.

Create a shaped seam allowance on a pattern after the piece has been drafted. Add hem and/or cuff allowance, then fold the hem or cuff in place just as the fabric will be folded on the garment itself. Add side seam allowances and cut out the pattern with the paper still folded. When the pattern piece is unfolded, you will see the shaping.

PIVOT

This term simply means keeping one point on a garment stationary while shifting the balance of the garment to another location. Pivoting is used in the process of copying garment pieces that have tucks and darts.

RIGHT SIDE UP

For a garment on which the left and right sides are dissimilar and that require separate pattern pieces, label the pattern pieces "right side up." This will tell you to place both the pattern and the fabric right side up for cutting.

PATTERN CODING AND STORAGE

EACH PATTERN PIECE should be labeled to help you identify it and use it correctly. Include the following information on each piece.

- The name or number of the garment as it is listed on the face sheet.

- The name of the piece itself, also as listed on the face sheet.

- Fabric from which the piece will be cut. Categories of fabric are described on page 14. It may be helpful to use a different color of ink to represent each kind of fabric. For example, you might use black ink to label pieces that will be cut from the main fabric, red for pieces to be cut from interfacing, blue for lining, and so on.

- Show the lengthwise grainline, for accurate laying out and cutting.

- If the piece is to be cut on a fold, use arrows to point to the foldline.

As you finish each pattern piece, cut a small hole near the straightest edge (so it won't catch and tear on the rod when it is put away), then simply place it on a garment hanger. This way you won't lose any pieces as you work on the pattern, and you will be able to find the finished pieces quickly. When the pattern is finished, cut a hole in the face sheet

and hang it in front of the pattern pieces. The pattern can be stored this way at the back of the closet, taking up very little space. And you will never have to press the pieces before using the pattern.

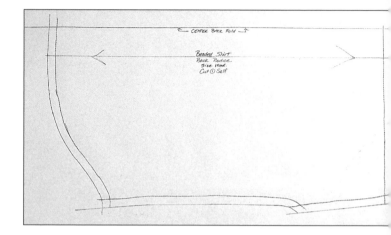

If you take a few simple precautions, your new pattern should last for years. Don't use pins to secure the pattern to fabric for cutting. They tend to distort the pattern and garment piece by pinching up the fabric, and can tear the pattern. Even if you cut with scissors instead of a rotary cutter, pattern weights are a better choice. They can be bought in a fabric or notions store. Assorted household objects can be used instead, as long as they don't get in your way when you are cutting. An inexpensive alternative to purchased weights is 35 mm film containers filled with sand.

To preserve your pattern, reinforce it with thin adhesive-backed vinyl. Fusible interfacing also works nicely when bonded to the back of the pattern pieces. Use a lightweight fusible and bond with a dry iron set at low heat. You also can transfer a paper pattern onto pattern-tracing fabric, but this is a more time-consuming process.

THE BLOUSE SHOWN below is used here to illustrate the steps in copying a garment and making a pattern. The style of the blouse is fairly simple, yet it has a good variety of components. Even if this garment doesn't resemble the garment you plan to use for your own first copying project, read through all of the steps just the same to learn the procedure. Details of other designs and constructions will be covered in later chapters.

COPYING A GARMENT: THE BASIC TECHNIQUES

GUIDELINES FOR MAKING A COPY

- Make the pattern pieces in the order they will be sewn, with each piece building on another.

- Begin with the back of the garment in most cases, since it usually will have fewer design features.

- Start with the largest section of the entire piece; for example, on a shirt with a back yoke, start with the lower back.

- If one side of the garment has more detail, copy that side.

- Write your own sewing instructions as you examine and copy each garment section. Make notes on the pattern pieces to help later in construction. Of course you can always refer to your original garment as well—providing you have kept it.

PREPARING A GARMENT FOR COPYING

Remove shoulder pads and any ornaments that will prevent the garment from lying flat and interfere with making a true copy. As only one side of the garment will be used for the copy, it will be necessary to remove the accessories only from that side. The copy will be made with the half of the garment that features the most detail. For instance, if a shirt has a pocket only on the left side, it is the left side that you will copy.

The garment should be freshly laundered and pressed. Wrinkles will prevent an accurate copy. A garment also can change shape when it is worn, as is the case with tight-fitting jeans. This can work in your favor, too. If the garment fits better after it has been worn, you may prefer to copy it that way.

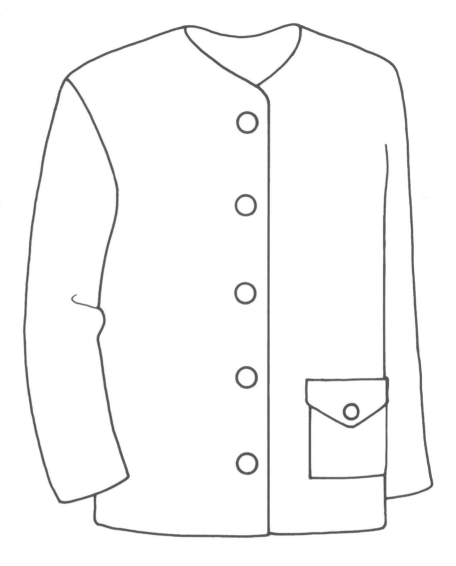

Copy the side of the garment that exhibits more style details.

THE GARMENT ANALYSIS

In looking at the construction of the blouse, we have observed the following details and made note of them: The front and back yokes are single layer. Both left and right front bands are separate pieces. French seams were used on the sides and shoulders, but we will use a serger to finish these seams and so will change the seam allowance accordingly. The sleeves are finished with 3/4-inch (2 cm) double hems. There is a 1/4-inch (.7 cm) double hem at the lower edge, which we will change to a 1/2-inch (1.5 cm) single hem. We won't duplicate the embellishment on this blouse, but the instructions for doing so can be found on page 106.

Before we begin, a face sheet will be made for the pattern as described on page 13. It will list the pattern pieces to be made, and indicate the number of each piece to be cut from each kind of fabric.

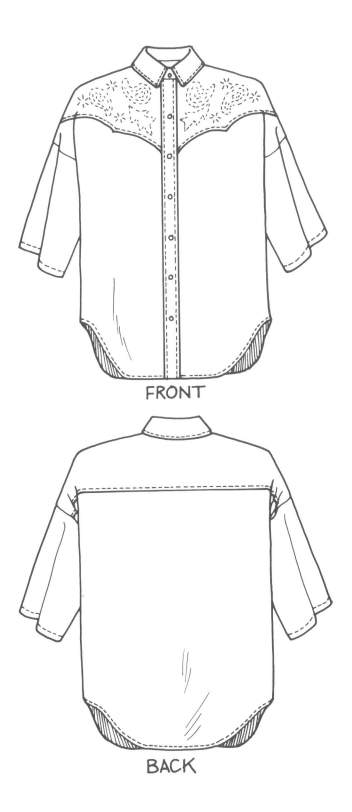

FRONT

BACK

BODICE BACK

Open the garment along the front, if possible, so that you are dealing with just a single layer of fabric. Fold the back in half and carefully place side seams together. Pin through both thicknesses of the garment along the seamlines to make sure the seams are lined up exactly. Mark the center back—the foldline— with pins or chalk, or simply with a crease. Then mark the center back of the yoke, the collar stand, and the collar in the same way.

Draw a line near one edge of a piece of paper to represent the center back. On this garment, as on most shirts and blouses, the center back line is also the lengthwise grainline.

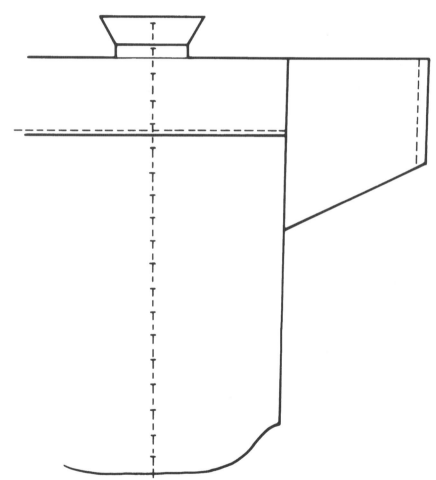

Mark the center of all back pieces.

Secure as much of the back, from center to side seams, as can easily be made to lie flat.

Use straight pins to secure the garment center back line to the line on the paper. If you had to fold the garment, place the very edge of the fold on the line. Turn the sleeve inside out to allow the garment to lie flat. Secure the rest of the garment back to the paper with pins, working your way around the back and smoothing the fabric as you go so the garment lies perfectly flat.

Keep pins out of the path of the tracing wheel.

Place pins outside the seams and away from edges so you will have ample room to run the needle-point tracer along the seamline itself. Take care not to pull or stretch the garment in any way or your copy will be distorted.

Isolate any area that will not lie flat.

If the back will not lie flat all the way to the armhole seam, you will need to "isolate" that remaining section to be copied separately after you have copied the rest of the back. To isolate an area, simply place a row of pins across at the point beyond which the garment seams will no longer lie flat.

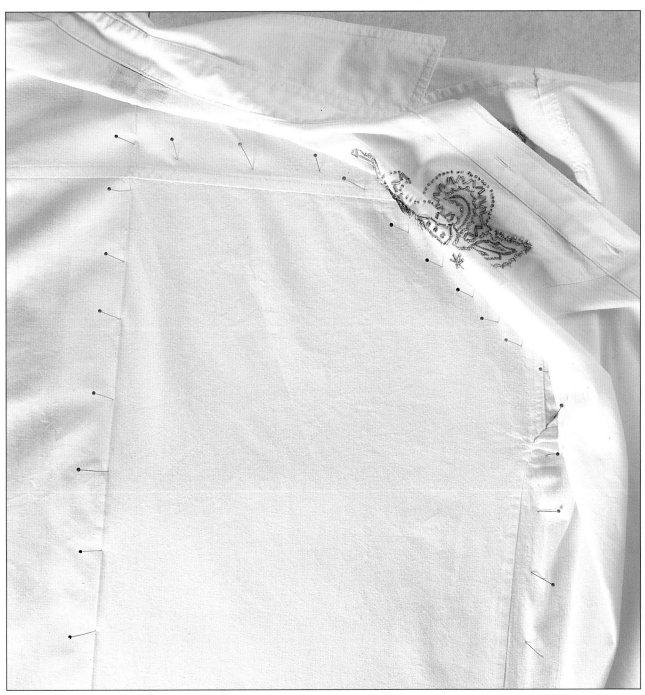

Transfer the outline of the secured section.

Run the needle-point tracer along the ditch of each seam, exactly where thread joins the two pieces. Use enough pressure to clearly mark the paper underneath. If the intersection of the underarm and bodice seams is too bulky to penetrate with the tracer, use a sturdy straight pin or pushpin and poke through to the paper below.

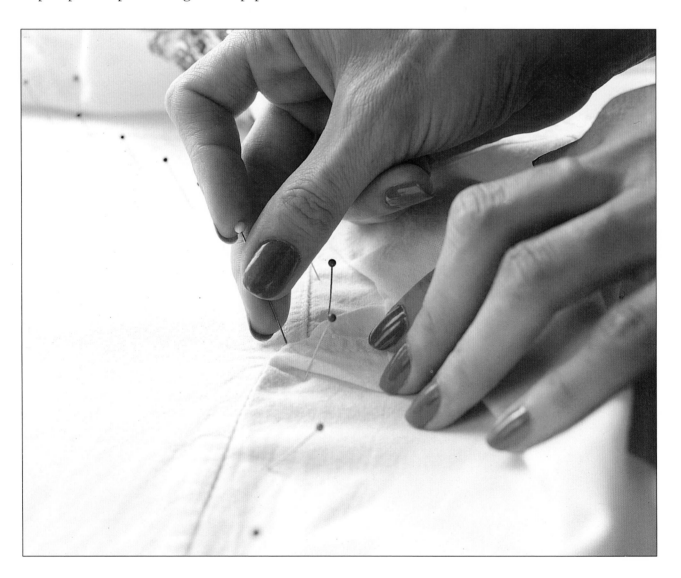

Extend each line slightly beyond the end of the seam.

Always run the tracer slightly past the garment edge or seam end to ensure a good clean intersection and to allow for the addition of seam allowances later. It will help eliminate guesswork.

Trace all the back seams with the wheel. Start and end at center back, so you will be sure no seam has been overlooked.

If the phone rings or you are suddenly taken away from the project, leave a piece of tape or other marker to remind you where you left off. If you do miss a section while tracing, do not try to realign it. It will not work. It is best to start over and retrace the whole piece.

Secure the isolated area and copy it.

Now you can remove the pins except for the row that designates the isolated area. Secure the remaining—isolated—area so it lies flat and trace that corner of the piece.

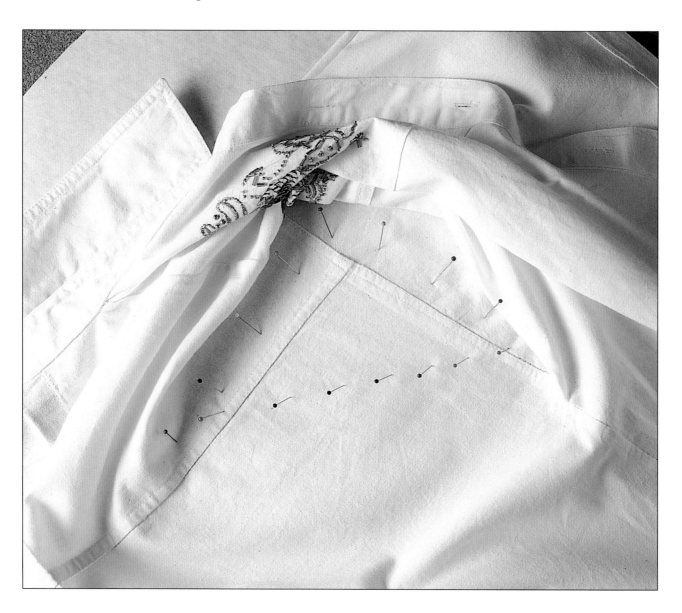

Draw in the seamlines.

Remove the garment and use a pen or pencil to draw along the outline made by the needle-point tracer. If you used the smooth wheel and carbon, the line should already be clearly visible.

Add seam allowances
to establish cutting lines.

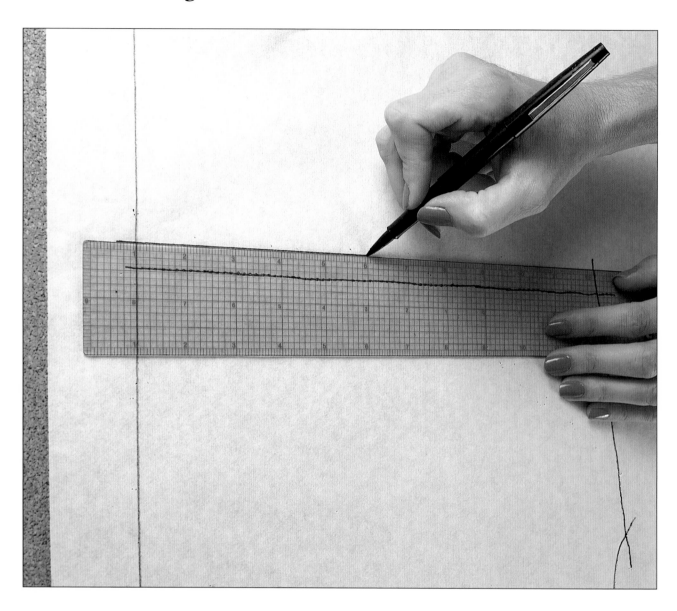

Use the clear ruler to add seam and hem
allowances to the outline, inching it
around the curves as you go. Straighten
any wavering lines.

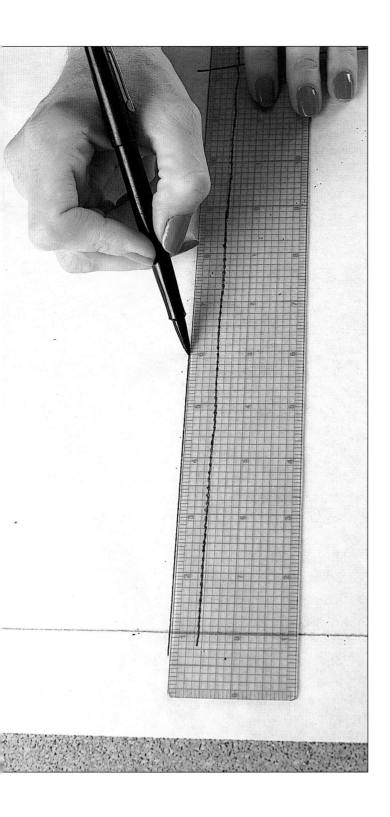

Square the yoke and hem with the center back line.

The upper edge and hemline of this garment should be at right angles to the center back—or lengthwise grain—line. Use the clear ruler or a carpenter's square to make sure they are correct.

Carefully cut the pattern piece around the outer edges. Label the pattern with the garment name, name of the piece, and other information as described on page 24.

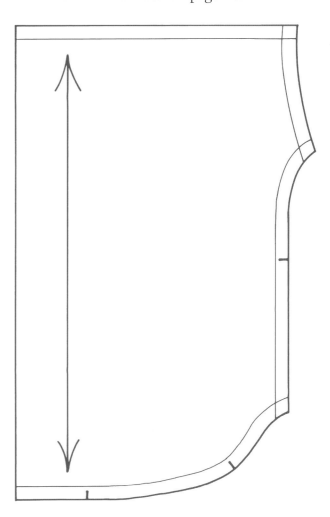

BACK YOKE

The back yoke is the next piece to be copied. Attached to the lower back bodice, it will complete the back of the garment.

Draw a line on a new sheet of paper to represent the center back and lengthwise grain, as before. Follow the same procedure used to copy the lower back bodice. When you add seam allowances, remember you have the option of using just 1/4 inch (.7 cm) at the neckline, and 1/2 inch (1.3 cm) elsewhere.

Check that the two back pieces match at the seamlines.

"Walk" the back yoke to the back bodice along the common seamline. Starting at the center back fold and ending at the armhole, carefully match the seamlines to make sure the pieces are even in length.

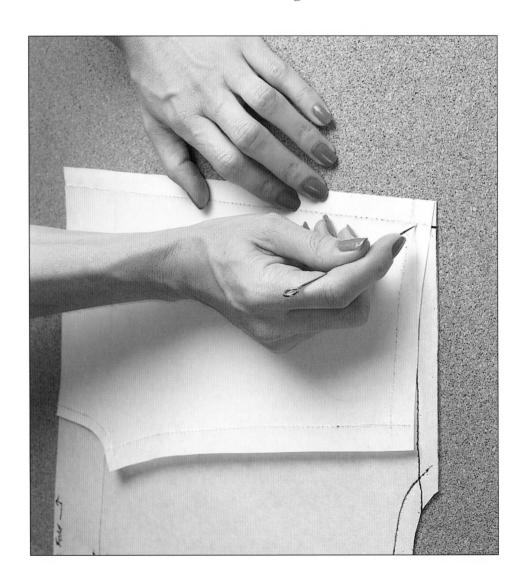

Adjust for discrepancies on adjoining seamlines.

If the seams are not the same length, measure the garment to see which is correct. If there is a discrepancy, adjust the appropriate pattern piece by blending a line to the correct point.

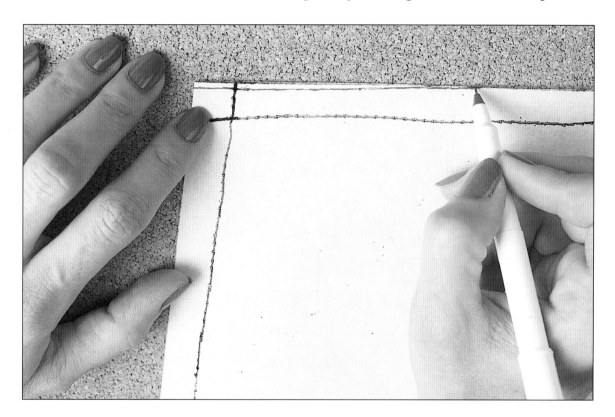

If the pieces differ considerably, you may have to retrace the incorrect piece. It is your call as to whether you should adjust the pattern piece or remake it. For example, a difference of 1/4 inch (.7 cm) on the length of a pants leg could be blended to match, whereas the same discrepancy on a small piece like a collar would be intolerable and the pattern should be remade. Consider the size of the piece against the amount of discrepancy. If you have followed the procedures correctly, the pieces should match up well.

Add notches
as matching points.

Mark a double notch (indicating a back pattern piece) somewhere along the common seamline on both back pieces. This will aid you in matching up the two pieces when you sew them together. When you cut the garment piece from fabric, also notch the center back of each piece.

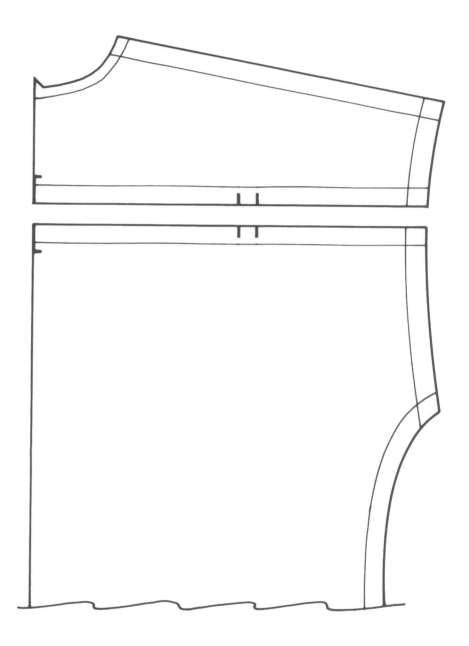

Measure the neckline to check the fit.

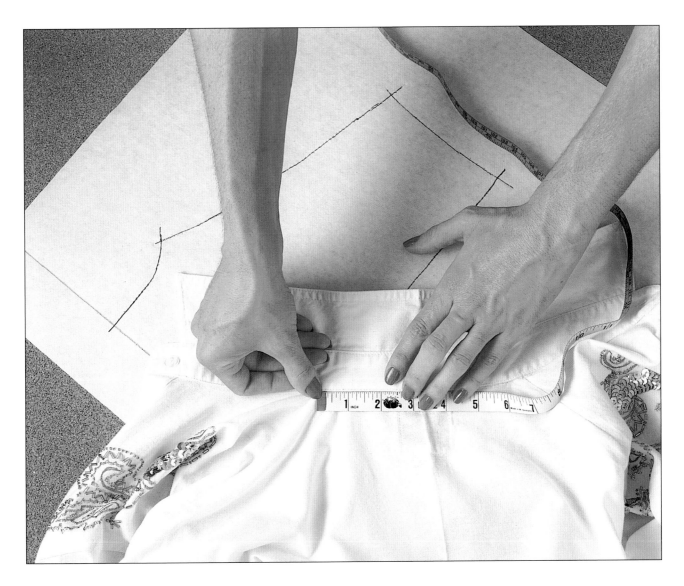

With the garment in a relaxed state, measure the back neckline of the garment and compare the measurement to that of the yoke pattern neckline. Pieces that are cut even slightly on the bias, as a neckline is, can easily be distorted. It is best to double check the pattern now to ensure that the collar and stand will fit correctly.

Label the pattern piece and set it aside.

BODICE FRONT

Start with the lower bodice, the larger front section. Follow the same procedure used for the back bodice. Remember to turn the sleeve inside out. Again, you may choose to add just 1/4 inch (.7 cm) seam allowance at the neckline and along the front where the band will be sewn.

Walk the bodice front to the bodice back along the side seams and make make any necessary adjustment. Label the piece and put it aside.

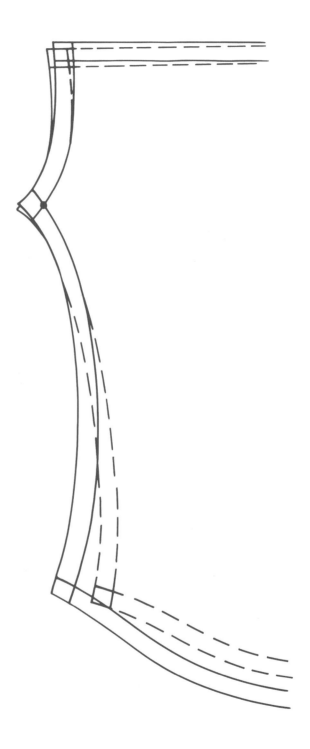

FRONT YOKE

Copy the front yoke according to the same procedure. Measure the pattern neckline against that of the garment as you did with the back.

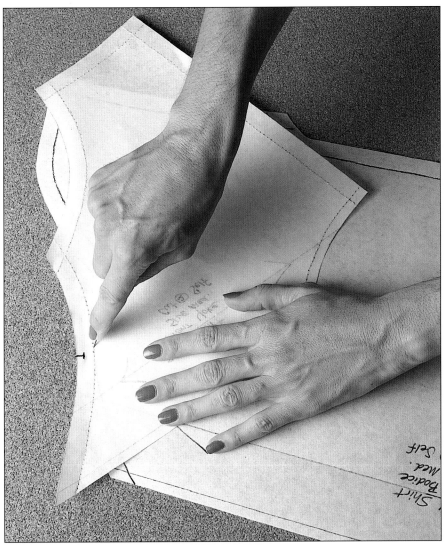

Walk the yoke to the bodice front pattern.

Because the yoke/front bodice seam on this blouse is shaped, the pattern pieces should be walked from the point at the center of the yoke piece outward toward the armhole, then from the point toward the center front. The reason for working outward in both directions from the center is that adjustment for any discrepancy should be made on both sides of the pattern rather than on one side only. It is critical to walk the pattern correctly along curved seamlines or the outcome will be wrong. Be sure to match the pieces along the stitching line, not at the outer edges of the seam allowance. Use a pencil or a pin to hold the paper in place as you shift the pattern while walking it along.

Allow for bustline ease.

If the bodice/yoke seamline is longer on the bodice pattern, do not automatically assume there is a mistake. Some bustline ease may have been added. You may have even noticed a slight puckering at the seam when you were making the copy.

You probably are already familiar with the areas in which you can expect to find ease. The amount of ease used in a garment can vary greatly, depending on the garment's fit and the fabric from which it is made. As shown in the photograph on page 70, a loosely woven cotton fabric eases more smoothly to a smaller piece of the same fabric than will tightly woven polyester.

If there is ease on your garment, make a notation on the pattern piece indicating where the ease can be found. This will be helpful when you assemble your garment.

Walk the front and back yokes together at the shoulder seamline. Add notches wherever you think they may be helpful.

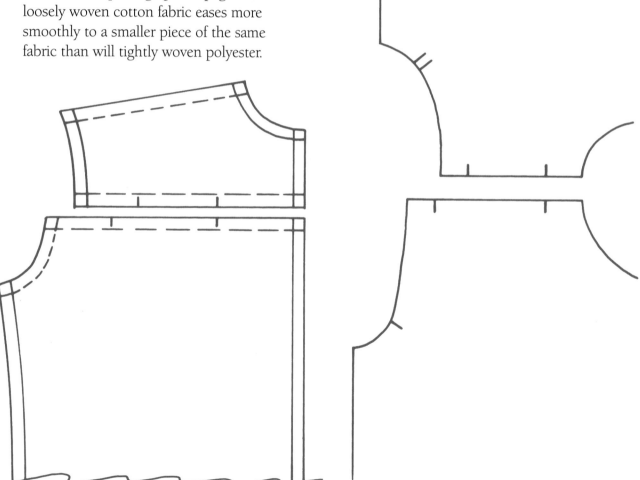

Place notches on the two adjacent seamlines to indicate beginning and end of an eased section.

SLEEVES

Work with half of the sleeve at a time to make the sleeve pattern. The back of the sleeve typically will be larger than the front. Since a sleeve is cylindrical, it would be impossible to copy the back without part of it rolling underneath and out of sight. Instead, fold the sleeve exactly in half lengthwise from the underarm seam to the center. It doesn't matter which is the back or front of the sleeve, or where the shoulder falls. Press in a crease, then pin along the fold.

Copy the first half of the sleeve.

Draw a line near the center of a piece of pattern paper. Pin the sleeve, front upward, with the fold along the line on the paper. You will find that the sleeve fold is also the lengthwise fabric grain in most cases. It helps to angle the pins, their heads away from the balance of the piece being copied. This will keep the piece from shifting as you pull against it to secure the remainder of the section. Secure the rest of the sleeve and copy the first half. Remember, you are tracing through two layers of fabric, so be sure to apply enough pressure to mark the paper. Add an occasional pin prick through thick seam allowances.

Mark the pattern for placement of notches.

With the tracer, mark across the seamline where yoke and shoulder seams meet the sleeve head so you can place notches at these points. These intersections will be critical when the sleeve pattern is walked to the bodice armhole. To distinguish between front and back when the sleeve is removed, place notches at the lower curve on each side of the sleeve cap close to the underarm seam where they won't be confused with the yoke notches. Use one notch on the front of the sleeve and two on the back.

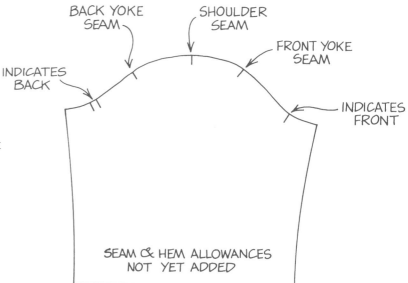

BACK YOKE SEAM

SHOULDER SEAM

FRONT YOKE SEAM

INDICATES BACK

INDICATES FRONT

SEAM & HEM ALLOWANCES NOT YET ADDED

Transfer the second half of the sleeve.

Unpin the sleeve and turn it over to copy the back. Start at the top of the cap. Again, match the fold to the line on the paper, and this cap seamline with the one already drawn.

Pin the balance of the folded edge along the line and secure the rest of the sleeve. Then complete the copy.

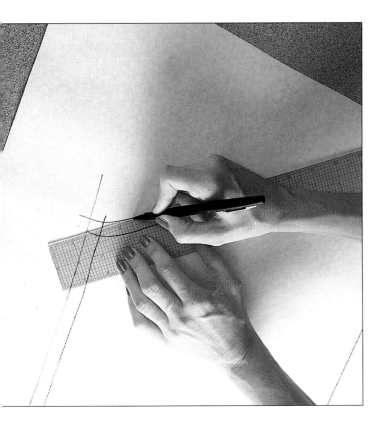

Walk the sleeve to the bodice.

When walking the sleeve to the bodice on a garment like this, start at the shoulder seam intersection and work in either direction toward the underarm seams. First walk it from the shoulder to the yoke intersection and correct the notch if necessary. Then continue to the underarm.

The sleeve cap is another area where you may find some ease. This shirt, however, has a dropped shoulder, so the ease has been eliminated. (A sleeve set into a fitted armhole will have ease at the cap. See page 71 for detailed copying information.) As you walk the bodice from the yoke to the armhole, mark the sleeve notches onto the corresponding points on the bodice.

There should be very little discrepancy when the sleeve is walked to the armhole. If there is a slight difference in the pieces, the sleeve seamline can be blended to match. If you have considerable trouble matching the pieces, it may be that the bias-cut part of the seamline was distorted when the sleeve was pinned in place. In this case you should draft a new pattern.

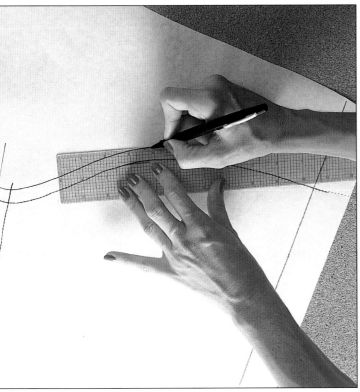

Use a see-through ruler to add seam allowance to the sleeve cap or other curved seamline. Draw a short line segment of the line— 1/2 inch (1.5 cm) or so—then reposition the ruler to draw the next segment. Continue this way around the cap.

Secure both grainlines
to copy an out-of-shape sleeve.

Keep in mind that the lengthwise grain runs the length of the sleeve, and the crossgrain is around its circumference. When you set up to make a new copy it may help to draw a second line at a right angle to the lengthwise grain line (the center of the sleeve) to line up the crossgrain of the sleeve fabric. Chalk or pin along the crossgrain of the sleeve from the upper point of the underarm seam across to the fold as shown. When you secure the sleeve, align it with both grainlines to make the copy.

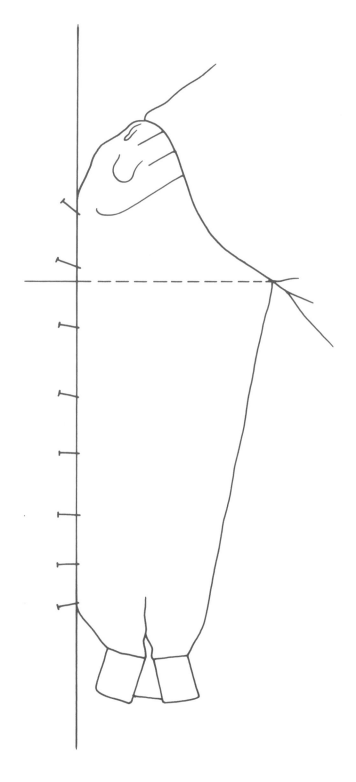

Add the hem allowance and shape the seam allowances.

When you add hem allowance at the lower edge of a sleeve that is not finished with a separate cuff, it will be necessary to shape the underarm seam allowances. To do this, first fold the hem allowance on the pattern just as the garment hem will be folded and sewn. Then add the underarm seam allowances and cut out the pattern piece with the hem still folded. When the pattern is unfolded, it will be shaped as shown.

The sleeves of this blouse have 3/4-inch (2 cm) doubled hems, so the total hem allowance added is 1-1/2 inches (4 cm).

If the sleeve is extended to create a self-folding cuff, it is especially important to shape the seam allowances. Make all the folds that constitute the cuff and hem and add seam allowances at the underarm seams. With the paper still folded this way, cut out the pattern piece.

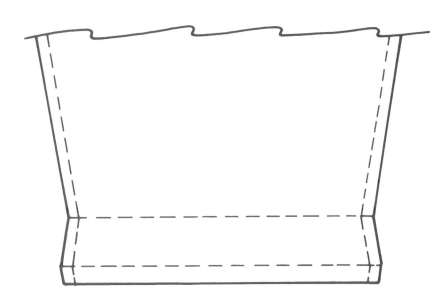

FRONT BANDS

The front bands are straight pieces: The easiest way to make the pattern for them is by taking measurements and then drawing the piece accordingly. The finished band for this blouse is 1-1/4 inches (3.2 cm) wide. The outer edge is on a fold, so the measurement is doubled to equal 2-1/2 inches (6.4 cm). A seam allowance of 1/4 inch (.7 cm) is added at each side for a total width of 3 inches (7.8 cm).

To make the band, draw two parallel lines on the paper, 3 inches (7.8 cm) apart and slightly longer than the finished band. Fold the piece in half lengthwise and trace just the neckline curve at the top of the band. Then mark the hemline at the lower edge. Add seam allowance at the neckline and hemline. Keep the piece folded as you cut it out to produce a shaped seam allowance at the neckline.

You may wish to mark button and buttonhole placement on the band. At least make a notation of the buttonhole spacing measurement for future sewing reference.

Cut a pattern piece for interfacing.

For the interfacing, make a separate pattern piece half the band width. If you will use fusible interfacing, it won't be necessary to add seam and hem allowances.

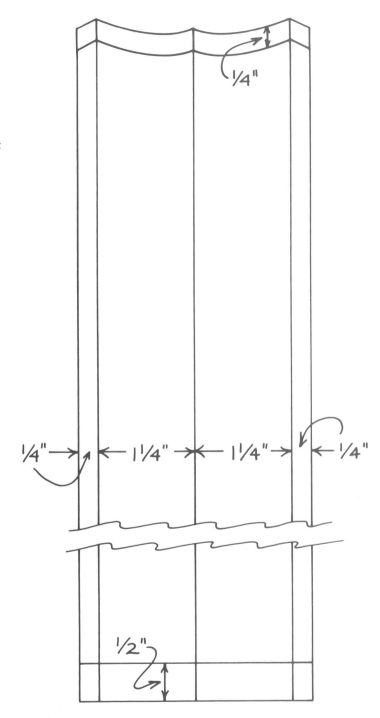

COLLAR STAND

Sometimes the collar and stand are made as a single piece, as shown in the drawing. In this case, the neck edge of the collar itself, rather than that of the stand, will be matched to the bodice neckline seam. Make a pattern for this kind of collar by following the shape and outline of the garment collar.

On our blouse, the collar stand is a separate piece. Once again, the piece is folded in half to find the center back. On the stand and collar, the center back line will be the crosswise rather than the lengthwise grainline. Collars and stands are cut with the lengthwise grain going around the neck for greater strength and minimal stretch.

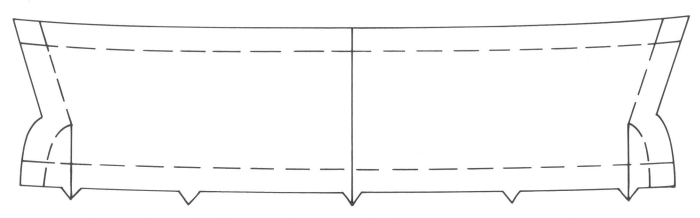

On our model shirt the collar and stand are separate, but the two sometimes are cut as a single piece.

Trace half of the collar stand.

Draw a line on the paper to represent the center back and place the center back of the collar stand, unfolded, along the line. If one side does not lie as well as the other, copy the better half. It is very important that you allow the balance of the piece to lie in its natural curved state. Place it flat without pulling or distorting the shape, secure it, and follow the standard copying procedure.

Add notches to the pattern piece.

Mark all important intersections with notches, such as the shoulder, band, and upper collar positions. It will be necessary to use pimple notches since only 1/4 inch (.7 cm) seam allowance will be added.

Even up the seamlines as you add seam allowance.

When you add the seam allowance you may notice that the piece widens or narrows in some places due to human error in the sewing. In the case of ready-to-wear, it's easy to forget that each garment was put together by a person sitting at a sewing machine just as you will be doing. The difference is that he or she was concerned with producing volume, while you are more interested in quality. Whenever you see a sewing error, you owe it to yourself to correct it as you make the pattern.

The collar stand should be even in width all the way across to the point where it curves to meet the front band. To correct the pattern, use the neckline as the stationary line and even up the band from center back to the front curved edge.

When you walk the stand to the neckline, start at the shoulder and work outward in both directions to the front edge and to the center back. Since you double-checked the neckline measurement when you made the bodice, any necessary adjustments will be made to the collar stand. This is an area where you should have very little discrepancy. Since the piece is so small, even 1/4 inch (.5 cm) difference is enough to warrant remaking the pattern.

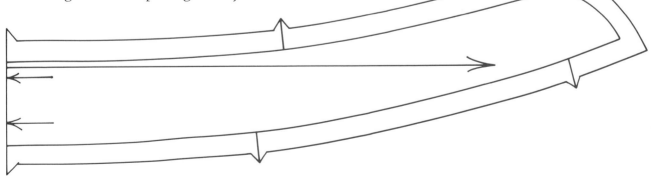

COLLAR

On this garment the upper collar and undercollar are the same size, with the seam exactly at the outer edge. It is a simple matter to improve upon the quality of the original garment by making the upper collar a bit wider at center back so that it will roll under slightly and conceal the seam at the collar edge.

Copy the collar according to the regular procedure. Walk it to the collar stand, making sure the pieces match up correctly at the ends. Use this pattern for the undercollar.

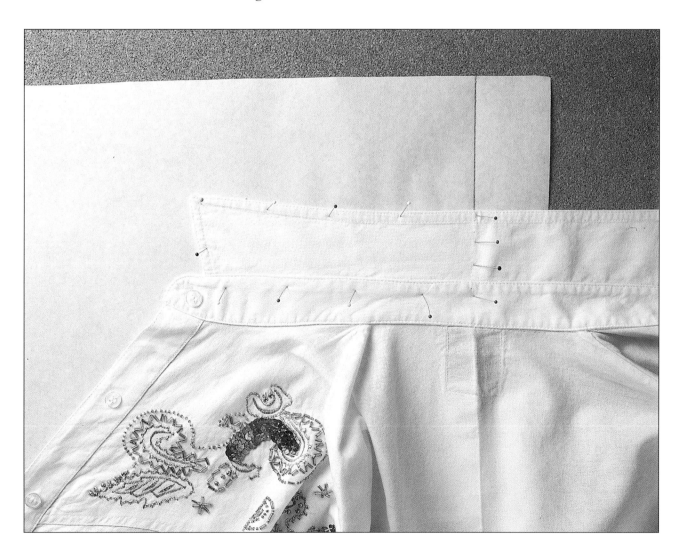

Draft the upper collar from the undercollar pattern.

Trace the undercollar, but don't ink in the outer edge seamline. At center back, measure out to a point 1/8 inch (.5 cm) beyond the traced outer edge. Keeping the collar point stationary, pivot the center back to the new point and draw in the collar outer edge as shown.

Use the upper collar pattern to cut sew-in interfacing. If fusible interfacing will be used, make a separate pattern piece, omitting the seam allowances.

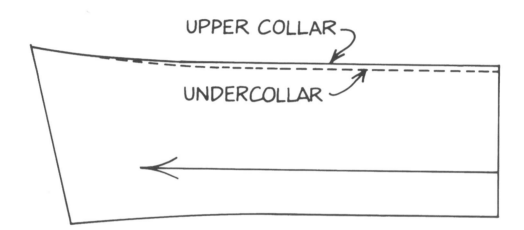

UPPER COLLAR

UNDERCOLLAR

THIS SECTION WILL familiarize you with the techniques used to copy the details that contribute to the fit and style of all kinds of garments. Garment styles may change constantly through the years, but many of the components never do. Once you understand how to copy the individual details, you will be able to deal with them, in any sort of combination, in your own patternmaking projects.

DARTS, TUCKS, AND PLEATS

These are the structural elements that shape and fit a flat piece of fabric to the three-dimensional human form. They can occur on almost any part of a garment.

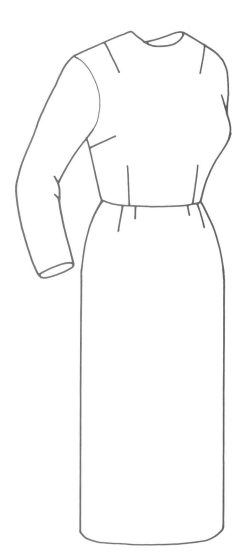

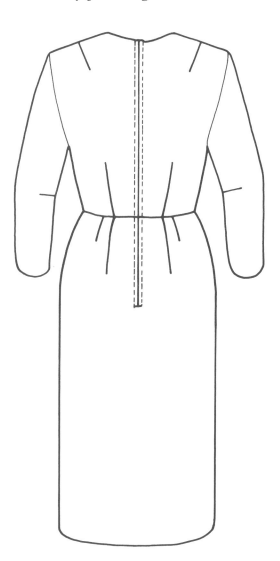

DARTS

A dart is a fold picked up in the material and stitched to a point at one or both ends. The stitching line of a dart can be straight or, on a shaped dart, will be curved.

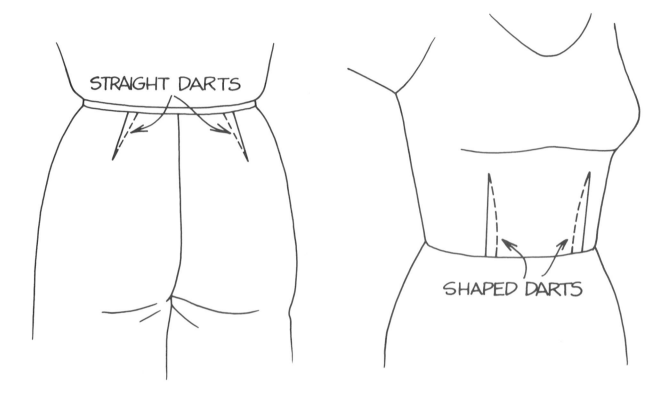

STRAIGHT DARTS

To copy a straight dart, first measure the depth of the dart from the stitching line to the fold at the dart's deepest point, which usually will be at the waistline or side seam. Make note of this measurement next to the listing for the pattern piece on the face sheet.

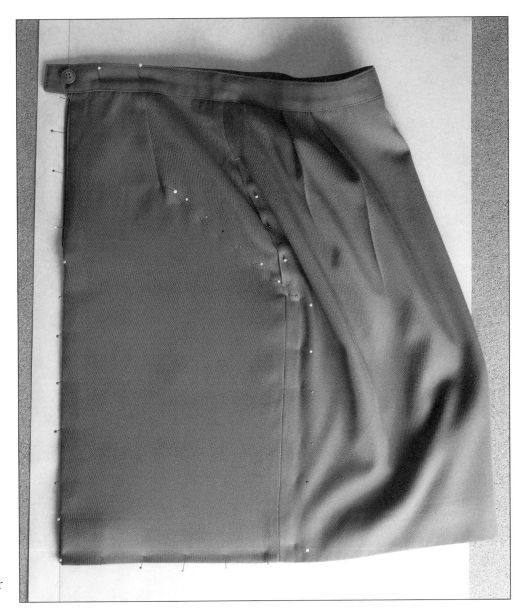

The copying technique will be the same for both vertical and horizontal straight darts. Begin by identifying the lengthwise grain on the garment front or back, as the case may be. Secure to the grainline as large a section of the garment section as can be made to lie flat. To isolate the three-dimensional darted area as shown, place a pin at the end of the dart. From that point, pin a line to the side seam. Note that this section will not lie flat.

Copy the garment section in the standard way. End by tracing a line down the first edge of the dart. Remove all pins except the row that defines the isolated area. Refer to the dart measurement taken earlier. Since the dart is folded in half, the measurement will be doubled for the total dart allowance. For instance, for a dart that measures 1/2" (1.3 cm), the total allowance will be 1 inch (2.5 cm).

Fold back the waistline to expose the first side of the dart. Measure across by the total dart allowance and mark that point. Secure the end of the dart with a pin as a pivot point, and shift the top of the dart over to the new mark. Secure the waistline and the balance of the garment, then copy the remainder of the piece.

Add a shaped seam allowance.

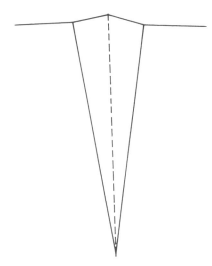

Mark for notches at the upper end of the dart, one on each stitching line. Mark the end of the dart 1/8" (.5 cm) from the actual point, toward the wider end. This way, the mark can be transferred to the fabric: It will not be seen since you will sew beyond it.

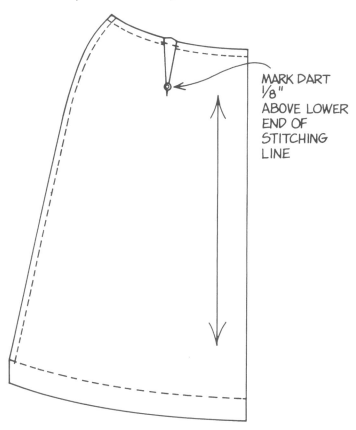

MARK DART 1/8" ABOVE LOWER END OF STITCHING LINE

Add the seam allowance, then fold the dart closed to shape the seam allowance. The folds of horizontal darts usually extend downward; the folds of vertical darts are toward the center of the garment. To fold the dart, first crease the side of the dart nearest the center of the garment. From the point of the dart, pivot it closed. Tape or pin the stitching lines together as if the dart were sewn. Blend a line to make the seam allowances meet in a smooth curve on the waistline and cut along the new outer line with the paper folded this way. When the pattern is unfolded, you will see the familiar peak that is a shaped seam allowance.

SHAPED DARTS

The procedure for copying a shaped dart is the same as for a straight dart, except that more measurements are needed because the stitching line is curved. Make note of each measurement on the face sheet. Start at the bottom and work up along the dart as shown, measuring the depth at regular intervals.

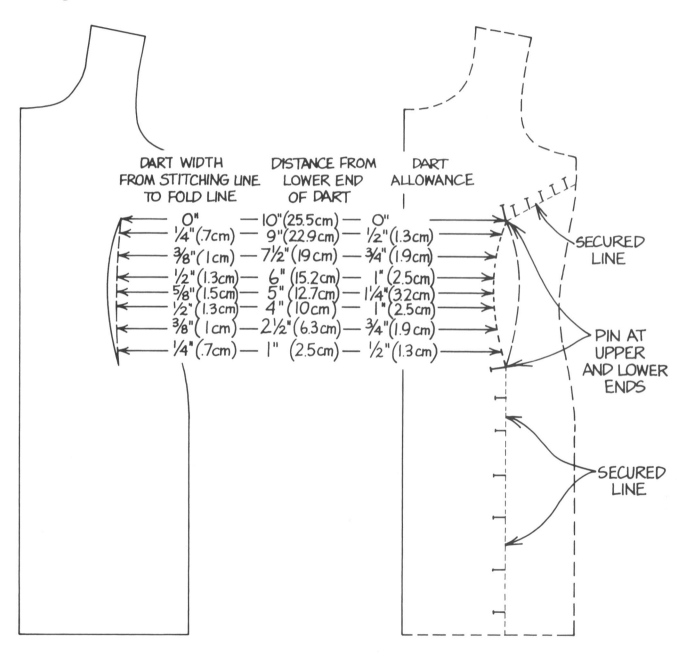

DART WIDTH FROM STITCHING LINE TO FOLD LINE | DISTANCE FROM LOWER END OF DART | DART ALLOWANCE

0" — 10"(25.5cm) — 0"
¼"(.7cm) — 9"(22.9cm) — ½"(1.3cm)
⅜"(1cm) — 7½"(19cm) — ¾"(1.9cm)
½"(1.3cm) — 6"(15.2cm) — 1"(2.5cm)
⅝"(1.5cm) — 5"(12.7cm) — 1¼"(3.2cm)
½"(1.3cm) — 4"(10cm) — 1"(2.5cm)
⅜"(1cm) — 2½"(6.3cm) — ¾"(1.9cm)
¼"(.7cm) — 1"(2.5cm) — ½"(1.3cm)

SECURED LINE

PIN AT UPPER AND LOWER ENDS

SECURED LINE

Copying a shaped dart

Copy the largest portion of the garment piece that will lie flat. Secure and isolate the dart area, pinning a line from the top of the dart to the side seam and from the bottom of the dart straight down. After the piece is copied, including the first dart seam, remove the pins except those defining the isolated area.

Lift the garment and mark the point to which the dart seam will be shifted, referring to the measurements. Remember to double each measurement to calculate the total dart allowance. Once you shift and secure the garment at the new points, it will lie flat and the copy can be completed.

To mark the dart for sewing, make a series of dots 1/8 inch (.3 cm) in from the actual stitching lines. These points can be marked directly onto the fabric since the stitching line will be 1/8 inch (.3 cm) outside the marks and will conceal the marks within the dart.

Occasionally the fold of a shaped dart will have been clipped away and you cannot shift using a measured dart allowance. If that is the case, you can either shift until the garment lies flat, letting the fabric grain guide you, or you may choose this occasion to let out the seam to expose the opening, allowing the fabric to lie flat with a hole in it. We have gone to extremes to avoid un-sewing, but sometimes it simply is the easiest way to work around a problem area.

TUCKS AND PLEATS

Tucks and pleats are essentially the same as darts, except that they are sewn closed only part way or not at all. For our purposes, if a fabric fold is sewn just across the top, it will be referred to as a pleat. A tuck is sewn part way along its length, and its depth must be measured both at the top and at the lower end of the stitched portion.

To copy a garment with pleats or tucks, first measure the depth and record the measurements. Mark the pattern paper for the lengthwise grain as usual, then draw a

perpendicular line through the first line to represent the crossgrain. On the garment pattern, the lengthwise grainline should not coincide with the tuck or pleat. If necessary, shift over to any parallel line and reestablish the lengthwise grain.

To secure the garment, choose a point on the lengthwise grain several inches below the tucks, up to which the garment will lie flat. From that point outward, secure the lengthwise grain and crossgrain as shown.

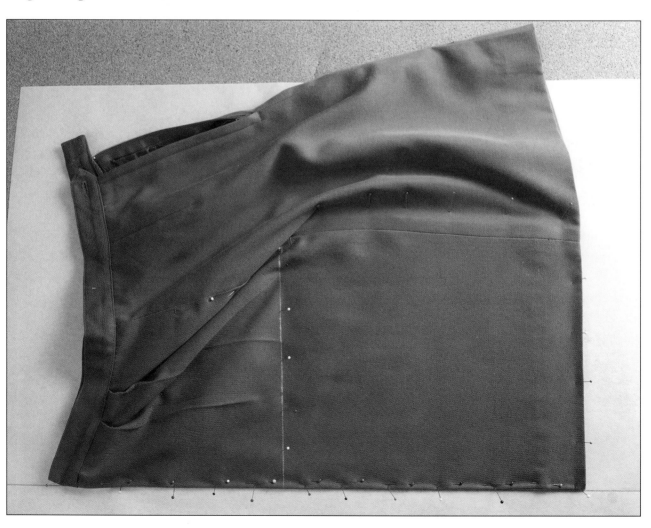

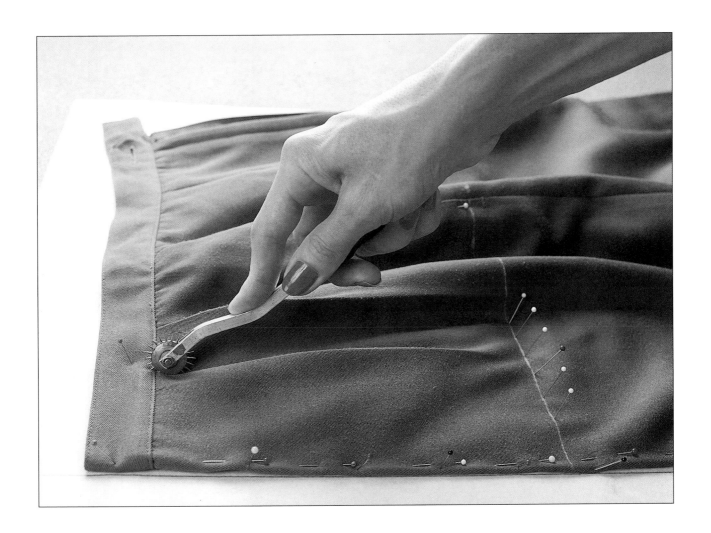

Copy the main portion of the garment piece in the standard way, keeping the tuck section isolated. On pants and skirts these details are most frequently found toward the hip. For that reason, you will want to work from the center of the garment out toward the side. In the isolated area, secure and continue copying the front until the first waistline tuck is reached.

Clearly mark the intersection of the tuck and the waist. Run the wheel along the ditch if the tuck is sewn down part way, then across the bottom to indicate where it ends. Check your notes for the depth of the tuck, then double the measurement for the total tuck allowance.

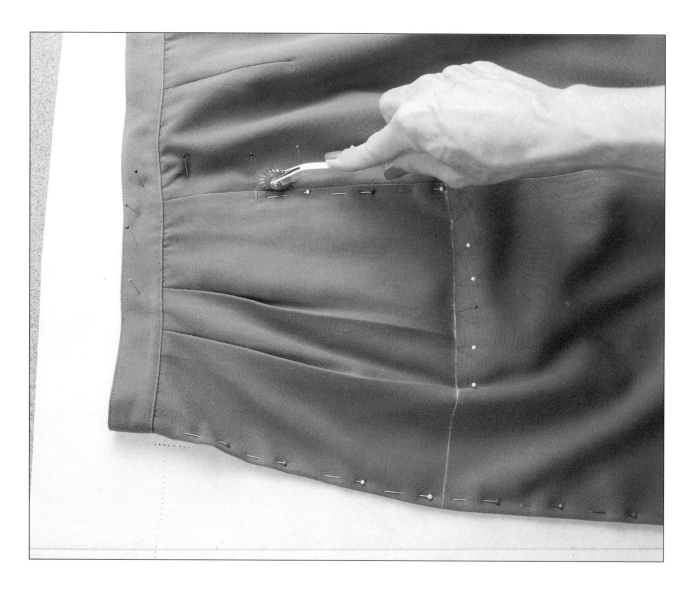

Remove the pins from the waistline and fold the garment back to expose the beginning of the tuck. Measure over the width of the total tuck allowance and make a mark at the waistline. If the tuck is partially stitched down, make a mark for the tuck allowance at the lower end of the tuck stitching as well.

Shift the tuck and secure it at the new position, then continue copying across the waistline to the next tuck. Again, release the waistline and mark the tuck allowance. Realign the garment shifting it over and securing it at the new position. The balance of the garment can be secured and copied now.

Add notches
and seam allowance.

Mark notches at the top of each tuck. Be sure to mark the lower ends of the tucks, too, if they are to be sewn part way down. Mark the end of tuck 1/8 inch (.5 cm) above the intended end of the stitching line. This way the marks can be transferred directly onto the fabric. Since the stitching will extend beyond the marks, they will not be visible. If you are marking pleats that will be caught only at the waistline seam, notches are necessary only at the waist.

Add seam allowance to the pattern. Fold the tucks as they will be sewn. Blend a line to make the seam allowances meet in a smooth curve on the waistline. While the pattern is still folded, cut the piece along the outer edge. This will create a shaped seam allowance, as you will see when you unfold the tucks.

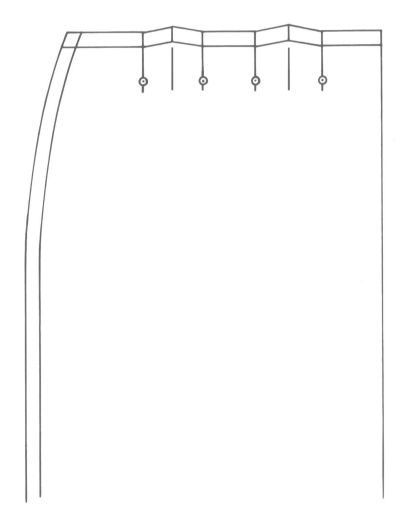

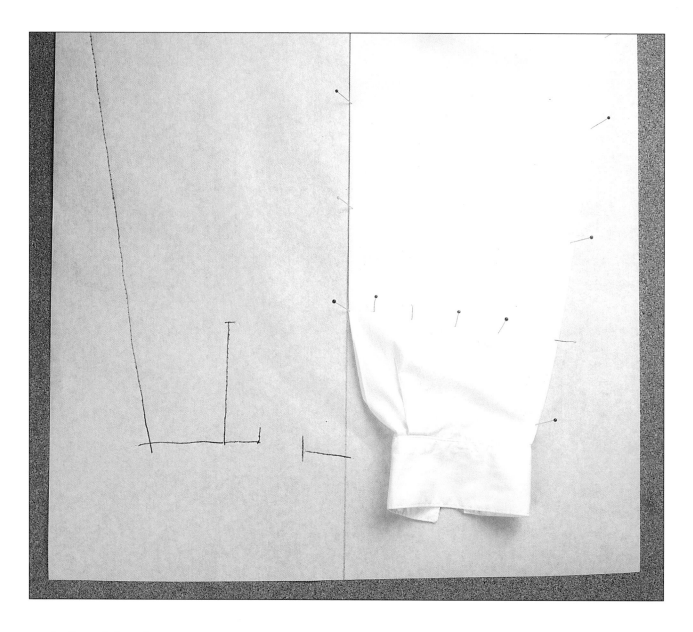

Tucks found elsewhere on a garment are copied in the same way as waistline tucks.

Secure and copy the largest possible area of the garment section, isolating the area of detail. Shift the garment by twice the measured tuck allowance, then realign it and continue the copy.

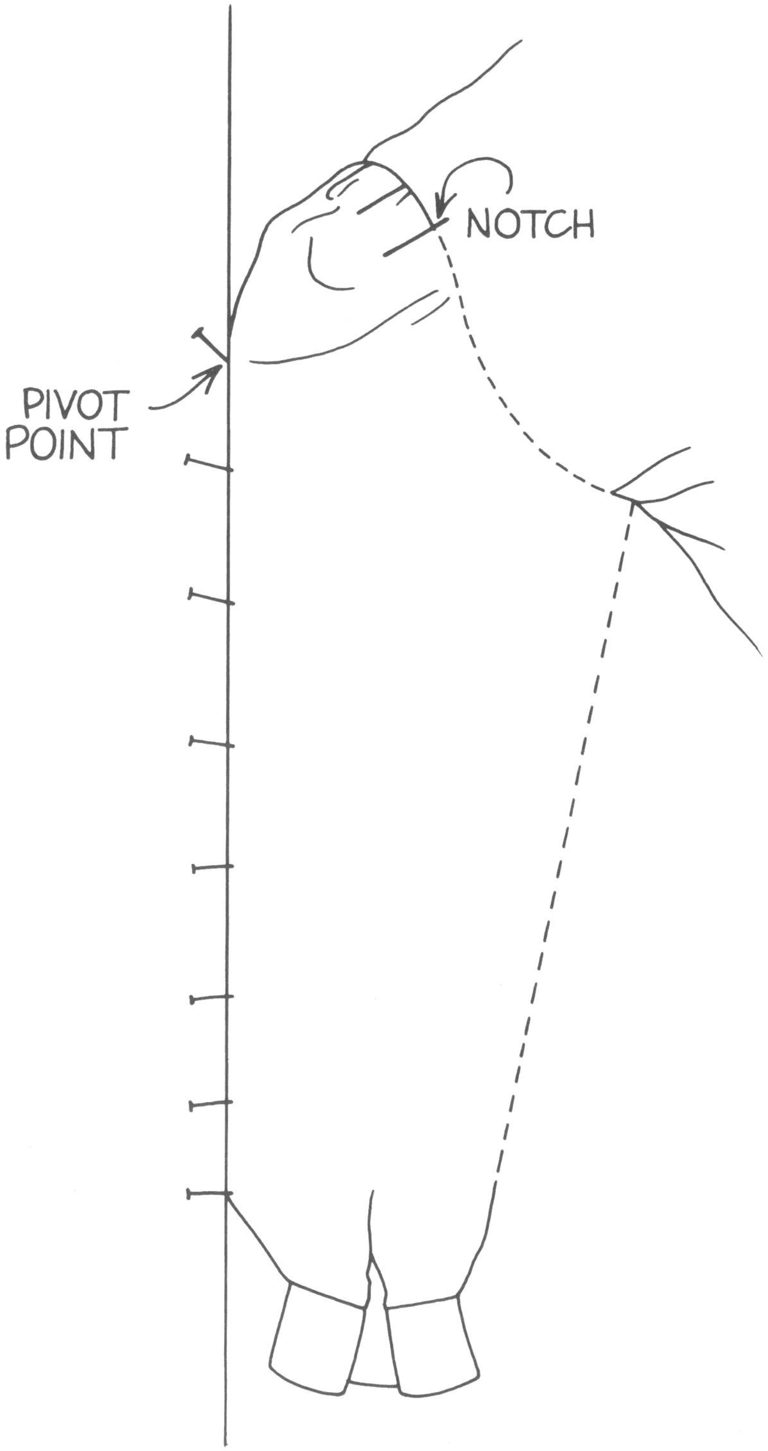

SLEEVE CAP TUCKS

The procedure for copying sleeve cap tucks is the same as that for waistline tucks. Secure the center fold of the sleeve up to the point where it will no longer lie flat. Next, copy the sleeve cap to the first tuck.

Remove all of the pins securing the sleeve except the pin closest to the cap on the fold. This pin will be used as a pivoting point. Measure across by the total tuck allowance. Pivot the sleeve and realign it at the new location. Continue around the sleeve cap until you reach the next tuck, then repeat the procedure. Continue measuring, pivoting, and realigning until you reach the center fold.

NOTCH

PIVOT POINT

Remove the sleeve, turn it over, and repeat the process on the other side. When the pattern piece is finished, fold in the pleats, in the direction they will be sewn, and tape them in place. Blend any lines that don't line up smoothly. Add seam allowance and cut the pattern with the pleats taped to create a shaped seam allowance.

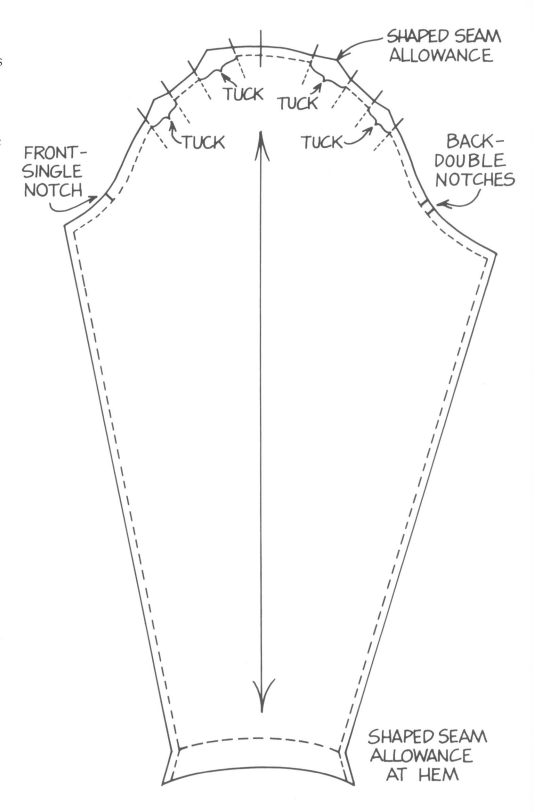

SHAPED SEAM ALLOWANCE

TUCK   TUCK

TUCK   TUCK

FRONT-SINGLE NOTCH

BACK-DOUBLE NOTCHES

SHAPED SEAM ALLOWANCE AT HEM

FULL-LENGTH PLEATS

If pleats extend the entire length of the garment—on a skirt for instance—the pattern paper can be pleated before the pattern is made. Fold pleats in the pattern paper, matching the width and spacing to that of the garment. Pin the pleats of the garment closed. Place the garment on the paper, garment pleats carefully aligned with the pleats in the paper. Then just proceed with the copy as if the pleats weren't there at all. Be sure to add seam allowance and cut the pattern while the paper is still folded so the seam allowance will be shaped correctly.

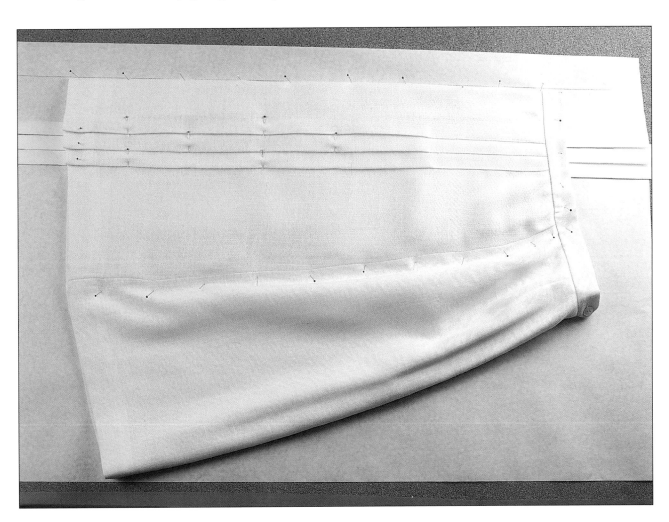

SHIRRING AND EASE

EASE, WHEN CORRECTLY SEWN, may not be visible. Gathers, on the other hand, are obvious. Nevertheless, the copying technique is essentially the same in either case: both involve attaching a larger piece of fabric to a smaller piece. The amount of ease, or shirring, can vary greatly, depending on the garment style and the fabric used. A loosely woven fabric will absorb more ease or shirring than will its tightly woven counterpart.

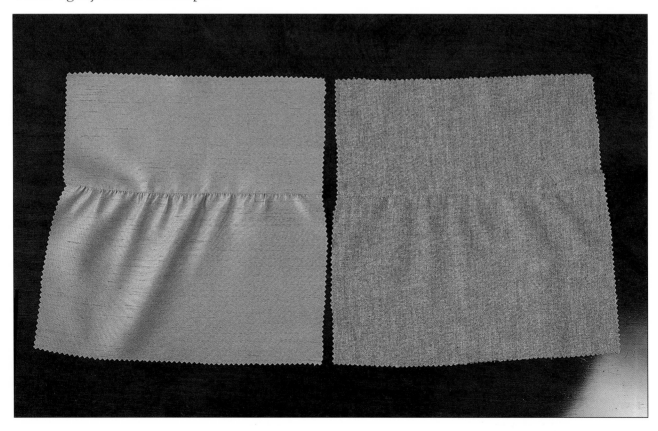

SLEEVE CAP EASE

TO COPY A SLEEVE with ease at the cap, follow the standard procedure for copying a sleeve, securing the fold of the sleeve up to the point where the cap will no longer lie flat because of the ease. Above that point, allow the cap to lie smoothly and to pull away from the center grainline. Trace the armhole seamline around to the fold at the center of the sleeve cap. Remove all pins except the one uppermost on the center fold, and shift the top of the sleeve over to the center line. Mark the top to give the total cap height. Blend a smooth curved line to connect the two points as shown.

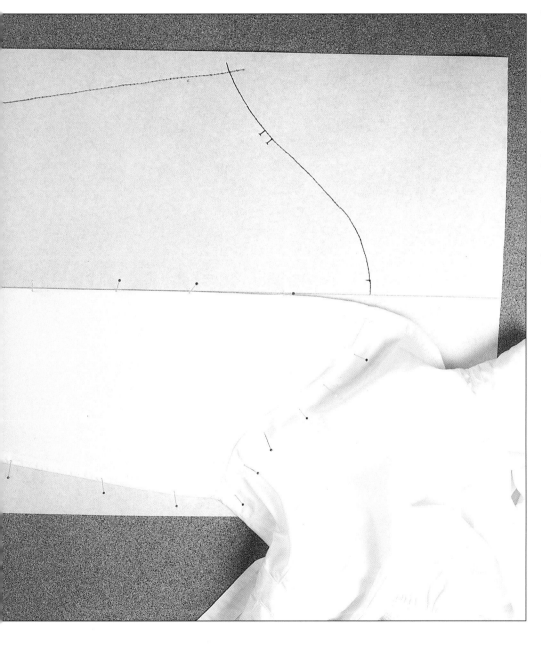

When you walk the sleeve to the armhole, start at each underarm seam and work your way to the shoulder. Add notches on the armhole to match the bodice to the sleeve when you sew. The excess on the sleeve is the ease and should be there. Do not remove it in order to make the two seamlines match in length.

SHIRRING AND GATHERING

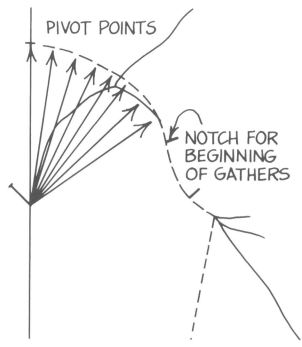

PIVOT POINTS

NOTCH FOR BEGINNING OF GATHERS

TO COPY A SLEEVE with shirring at both cap and wrist, secure the center fold to the grainline only as far as you can manage to lay the sleeve flat as shown. Use the last pin at each end of the fold as a pivot point. Copy the cap first, shifting a little at a time, inching your way across to mark the paper below. End at the center fold, the highest point of the cap. The marks can be blended to create a smooth cap line as shown.

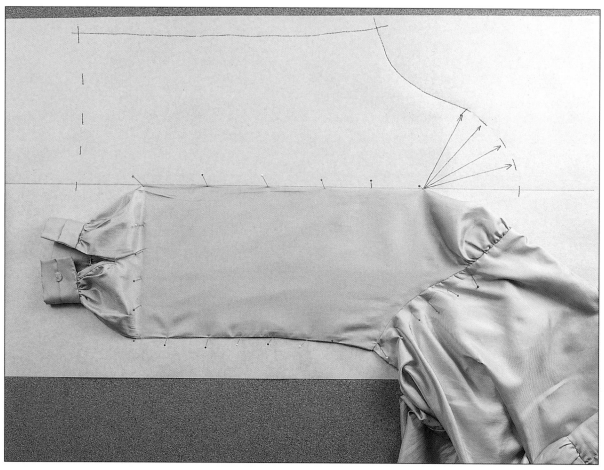

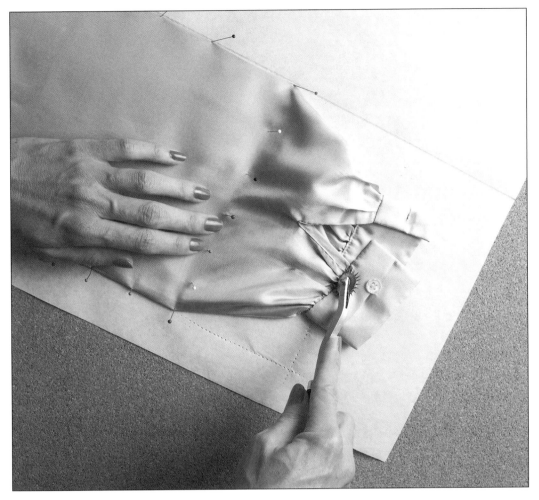

At the wrist, secure a line across the sleeve at the point where the sleeve will no longer lie flat. Slowly work across the cuff seamline, running the tracer along the ditch. Shift and relocate the cuff as you work toward the center fold. It may be necessary to release some of the pins from the secured line in order to work your way across. This is fine as long as you don't remove any pins from the point directly above the section you are still copying. Ending at the center fold, mark for the fully extended length of the sleeve. Link the dots to create a smooth line at the bottom of the sleeve.

Shirring on a skirt or blouse would be handled in the same way. Secure the section and shift, marking along the ditch. Inch your way along the seam, then connect the dots to create a smooth seamline.

Add notches on the seamlines of this piece and the adjacent one to indicate where the shirred area begins and ends. Note on the pattern that the piece is shirred or eased between the notches.

SLEEVES

THE BASIC TECHNIQUE for copying a plain set-in sleeve was described in detail beginning on page 45. Sleeves with ease, shirring, or tucks are discussed under those headings, beginning on page 67. That leaves just a few sleeve styles to consider here.

SLEEVES WITH ELBOW EASE

Fitted one-piece sleeves sometimes have added ease in the elbow area of the back seam to allow freedom of movement. Most clothing today is cut generously, eliminating the need for ease at this point. One exception is the narrow sleeves found on traditional wedding gowns. Without the added sleeve ease, the bride would be unable to put her arms around the groom!

When elbow ease has been added, the sleeve will hang with a slight curve, bending toward the front of the body. In some fabrics, there may also be detectable fullness or a slight puckering at the back elbow.

There are two ways to copy a sleeve that has ease. One option is to open the sleeve seam from just above the elbow to the lower edge. Carefully press the fabric into shape, then copy the sleeve according to the standard procedure.

The second method does not necessitate resewing the seam. Begin by securing the sleeve back from the cap to a point a few inches above the elbow. (Note that a sleeve with ease at the elbow is also likely to have ease at the sleeve cap. The procedure for handling cap ease is explained on page 71.)

Next, secure the eased area as a dome-shaped line: Pin just a 1-inch (2.5 cm) section, and transfer the seamline that corresponds with it. Secure the next 1-inch (2.5 cm) section, removing pins from the first section, and transfer that line. Continue this way along the dome-shaped line. Smooth the seamline you created in the transfer.

Place notches above and below the eased area. Transfer the notches to the sleeve front seamline by walking from the armhole down to the upper notch, then from the wrist up to the lower notch. The difference in length of the two pieces, between the notches, constitutes the fabric that will be eased in when the seam is sewn.

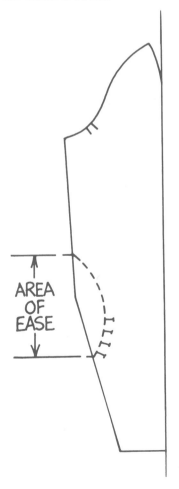

AREA
OF
EASE

74

TWO-PIECE SLEEVES

A two-piece sleeve, like a sleeve with elbow ease, also will bend slightly toward the front of the garment. It is copied in three steps.

Copy the upper sleeve first. Fold it in half on the lengthwise grain and proceed as for copying any one-piece sleeve. Pin across the lengthwise seamlines for notches above and below the elbow and transfer the marks to the pattern paper. There may be ease in this area and the notches will help you match up the pieces later. Turn the upper sleeve over and realign it on the grainline to finish the copy.

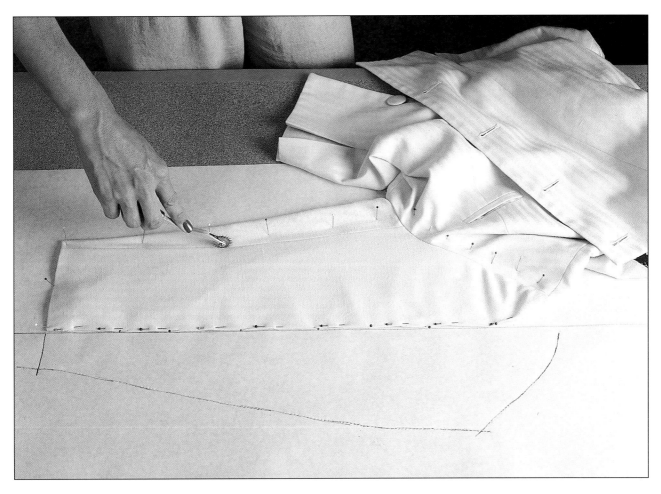

The undersleeve can be copied all at once. Establish the grainline and secure the section flat through all layers of fabric. Copy it in the standard manner. Remember to transfer the notches above and below the elbow. Place a notch, too, at the intersection of the sleeve and the bodice side seam.

When you walk the undersleeve to the upper sleeve to match the pieces, start at the top of the sleeve and work downward to the notch above the elbow. Then start at the lower edge and work upward to the notch below the elbow. Between the notches the upper sleeve may be longer due to added ease. Don't attempt to make the pieces the same length at this point.

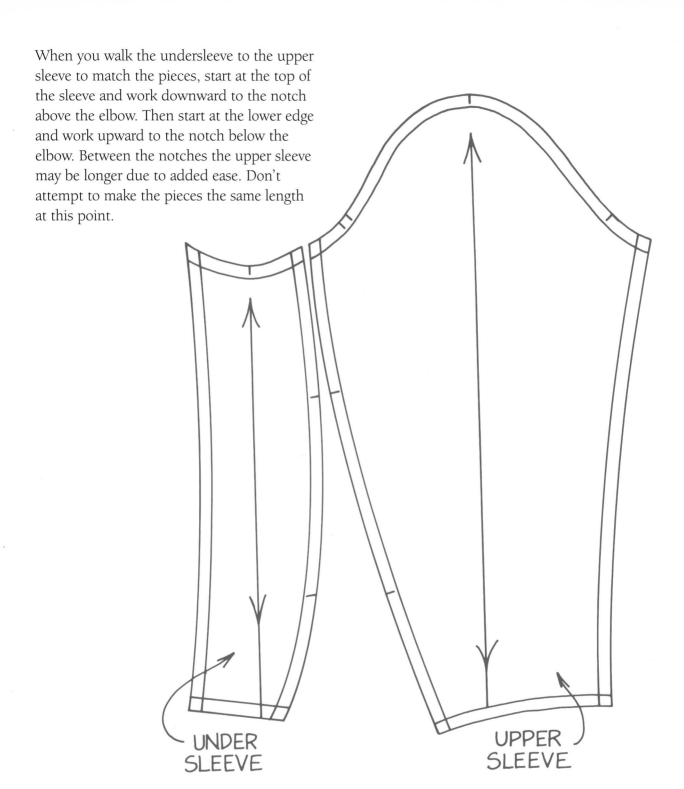

UNDER SLEEVE

UPPER SLEEVE

ONE-PIECE RAGLAN SLEEVE

Raglan sleeves are constructed in several different ways. The copying procedure varies slightly for each style.

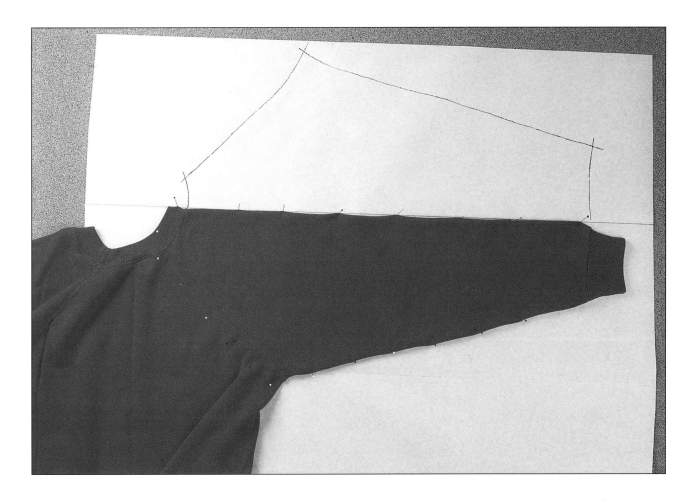

The easiest variety to copy is a one-piece raglan without a shaped shoulder, the type usually associated with a basic sweatshirt. To copy this sleeve, simply fold it in half from the underarm seam and pin the center fold in place. Secure the fold to the grainline on the paper and copy according to the standard procedure. Turn the sleeve over, realign it on the paper, and copy the other side. The shoulder seams are on the bias, so take care not to stretch or distort them as you secure the garment. Mark for placement of notches in the armhole and at the top of the shoulder, and transfer them to the bodice pattern pieces.

TWO-PIECE RAGLAN SLEEVE

Another raglan style features a shoulder seam that may or may not continue down the arm. For a two-piece sleeve with a seam along the arm, begin as usual with a line on the paper to represent the lengthwise grainline.

You will have to follow the yarns on the sleeve front and back to find the fabric grain because the overarm seam may have a slight curve to it. This curve provides additional ease.

The front sleeve can be copied in one piece. Secure the grainline first, then pin the rest of the sleeve in place. Copy the piece in the regular way. Place a pin across the seam in the armhole and another at the top of the shoulder curve. Place notches at these locations on the pattern. Then transfer the notches to the bodice pattern.

The back sleeve is larger than the front, so it must be copied in two sections. To start, establish and pin a fold along the lengthwise grainline somewhere near the middle of the back sleeve. This technique is similar to that used to copy a dolman sleeve, illustrated on page 80.

Draw a line on the pattern paper and secure the fold of the sleeve to the grainline. Copy it according to the standard procedure. Mark notches as for the sleeve front. Turn the sleeve over, aligning it with the grainline and matching it at the top and bottom. Repeat the process to complete the back sleeve.

When you walk the overarm seam of the front to that of the back, the two should match from the wrist to the shoulder. From the curve at the shoulder to the neckline, however, there may be ease on the back sleeve. If the back sleeve is approximately 1/8 inch to 1/4 inch (.5 cm to 1 cm) longer than the front, leave it as it is and ease in the excess when you sew.

Remember to shape the seam allowance on the hem if there is not a cuff. Follow the instructions on page 23.

ONE-PIECE RAGLAN
WITH A SHAPED SHOULDER

A raglan sleeve with a seam on the shoulder that does not extend down the overarm also is copied in three sections.

Pin or mark the lengthwise grainline from the end of the shoulder seam to the bottom of the sleeve. Follow the threads, if necessary, from the shoulder to the wrist to locate the grainline. Match the marked center sleeve grainline to the line on the pattern paper and copy the front sleeve.

Place pins across the seam in the armhole to locate notches on the pattern. Remember to transfer these notches to the bodice pattern.

Since the back sleeve is larger than the front, you cannot lay it flat without part of it rolling underneath where you cannot see it. For this reason, the back must be copied in two sections.

On the back sleeve, mark a grainline parallel to the one previously marked. Measure the distance between the two lines. Use the measurement to draw a corresponding parallel grainline on the paper. The second line on the paper will represent the back sleeve grainline. Align the back sleeve to the front sleeve at the end of the shoulder seam. Secure it along the center sleeve grainline to the bottom of the sleeve. Smooth it out and pin it to the parallel grain line on the back sleeve. Copy the section up to the back grainline.

Remove the pins and roll the front sleeve under the back sleeve section so that the back sleeve will lie flat from the back grainline to the underarm seam. Secure the back grainline to the corresponding grainline previously drawn on the pattern, matching it up at top and bottom to continue the lines. Then copy the balance of the back sleeve to complete the piece.

The back shoulder seam may be longer than the front due to ease that should be found there. If the back sleeve is approximately 1/8" to 1/4" (.7 cm to 1 cm) longer than the front, leave it as it is and ease in the excess when you sew.

If the sleeve has a hem at the lower edge rather than a cuff, shape the sleeve seam allowances in the manner described on page 23.

Dolman and Kimono Sleeves

Dolman sleeves and kimono sleeves are simply extensions of the bodice. They are very easy to copy and basically self-explanatory with one exception: The back is larger than the front and will roll under to hide one of its seams from view. As with any other garment segment in which not all of the seams are visible when the piece is laid flat, the section will have to be divided and copied in two sections.

With dolman and kimono sleeves, the back shoulder will have to be copied as a separate section. To do this, create a realignment point on the crossgrain. Identify the center of the bodice, then mark a line on the crossgrain to divide the piece in two. Mark the crossgrain line on the garment a few inches down from the point where the shoulder seam rolls underneath. Mark the lengthwise and crossgrain lines on the paper as well. Then secure the bottom section of the garment to both grainlines. The shoulder seam will roll

out of sight under the garment. Copy the piece up to the crossgrain position as shown.

Release the garment and realign it on both grainlines to continue from the point where you left off. You can now secure the balance of the piece, previously hidden underneath, and complete the copy.

If the sleeve is hemmed, remember to shape the seam allowances as explained on page 23.

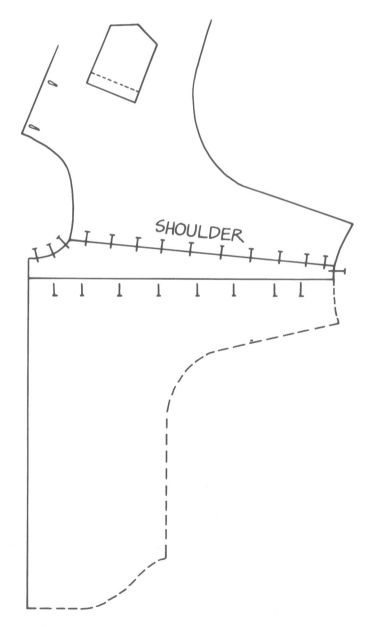

PANTS LEGS are shaped like cylinders. Technically, the front leg could be copied as one piece, since all seams are visible when the piece is laid flat. The back leg, larger than the front, must be divided into two sections for copying. The copying procedure is similar to that used for a sleeve—another cylindrical shape. It is preferable to copy both back and front legs in the same manner. The front leg often features style details such as tucks or pleats that are easier to copy with a smaller body of fabric to shift.

Begin with the leg that has the greatest number of style details. For instance, there may be topstitching for a fly zipper on the front, or there may be a pocket on one side of the back. Refer to the sections on tucks (page 62), pockets (page 84), or darts (page 56) if your garment has these style details.

Identify the grainline on the leg by matching the seams from the hem up to the knee. Pin through both layers of fabric along the center fold. Extend the grainline up the leg to the waist. If the grainline interferes with a style detail such as a tuck, relocate it on any parallel grainline to divide the leg into flat or detailed sections.

If you are working with a lightweight fabric that shifts off grain easily, it is a good idea to establish the crossgrain as well. Fold the garment at a right angle to the lengthwise grain, across the widest point of the crotch at the top of the inseam. Pin or mark this line. Prepare pattern paper with both lengthwise and crosswise grains indicated. Secure the pants leg to both grainlines before you start the copying procedure. For details on dealing with a garment that has developed baggy knees, see page 18.

Sometimes a pants leg will tend to twist, a sure indication that it was cut slightly off grain. Oddly enough, the trouble usually is with just one leg of the pair. The other leg, then, is the one from which to make your pattern.

Place pins across the seam at the knee and hip for notches. Draw the lengthwise grain on the pattern paper. Secure the fold of the leg to the grainline as shown. Smooth out the garment and secure it at the waist and down the seam. Copy it in the normal fashion.

Turn the leg over and realign it on the grain-line, matching the waist and hem. Continue copying from the point where you left off. Take care not to distort the bias curve of the crotch area; this is the key to a correct fit.

Create shaped seam allowances at the hem as described on page 23. If the waist edge folds to the inside to form an elastic casing, shape the upper seam allowances in the same way.

POCKETS

A POCKET IS not merely functional; a cleverly designed pocket also can add an element of interest to almost any garment. Take time to draft your pocket patterns neatly and accurately.

PATCH POCKETS

Patch pockets are sewn onto the outside of the garment. When you copy a garment section with a patch pocket, mark each of the pocket corners on the pattern paper with a pinhole. Then make the pocket pattern after you have removed the garment section from the paper. Since patch pockets on manufactured garments are sewn speedily, therefore not always perfectly, it is best to draft your own pattern using the finished pocket as a guide to size and placement. A pocket should adhere to the grainline of the garment section where it is placed.

To mark pocket placement on the garment, place a dot 1/8" (.7 cm) in from each corner. The marks will be hidden when the pocket is sewn in place.

RECTANGULAR POCKET

To make the pocket pattern, first draw a line to connect the pin marks at the upper corners of the pocket. Draw lines from the upper corners at right angles to the top to create the sides, extending them beyond the deepest point of the pocket. Create a box by adding the bottom line at a right angle to the sides across the deepest point of the pocket. You now have a balanced four-sided pocket and can stop here

if you wish. Add hem allowance at the upper edge and seam allowance on the other sides. Label the pattern.

POCKET WITH ROUNDED CORNERS

For rounded lower corners, first cut the pocket pattern piece as a square. Outline one corner curve. Fold the pattern in half lengthwise, and transfer the corner curve to the other lower corner for a mirror image. If you like this shape, make a template of stiff paper for future use.

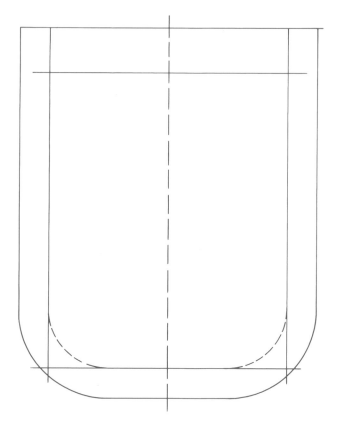

FIVE-POINT POCKET

The same square can be used to draft a traditional five-point pocket. Make sure both sides are exactly the same length. Mark the center point of the top and bottom line, and draw a line connecting the two centers, extending the line downward to the desired point. Connect this point with the lower corner on each side.

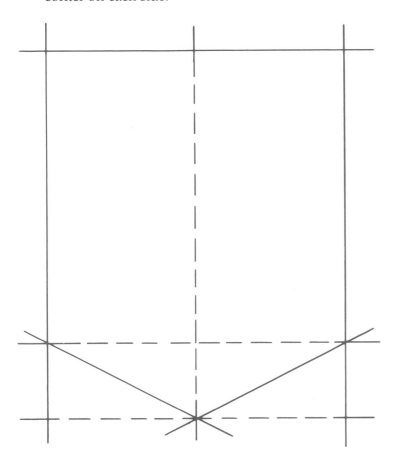

INSEAM POCKETS

On some garments, a pocket in the side seamline is cut as an extension of the side of the garment. This is a case in which it is easy to improve the quality of the garment when you copy it by cutting the pocket pieces separately and stitching them to the side seam allowances.

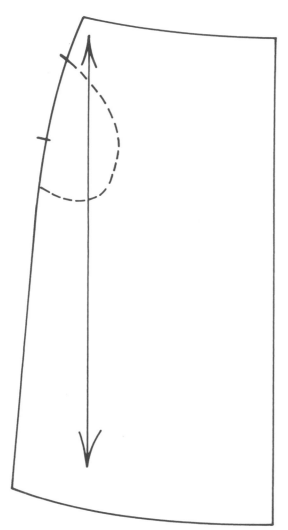

Begin by pinning the pocket opening closed. Pin through the garment along the pocket seamline or fold, creating a pinned outline on the outside of the garment. Transfer a parallel grainline from the body of the garment onto the pocket area.

Copy the body of the garment first. On the side seam, mark the top and bottom of the pocket opening. As long as the pocket section doesn't include any special style details, such as tucks or gathers, the pocket line can be transferred directly through to the pattern for the body of the garment.

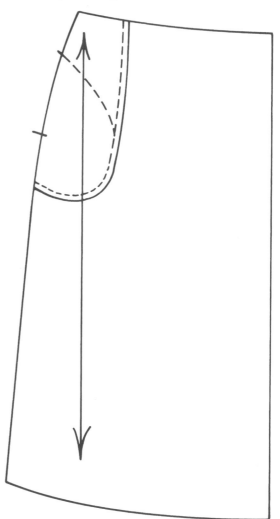

To make the inner pocket pattern piece, place pattern paper over (if you can see through it) or under the pocket area and copy the finished pocket lines.

If there is a style detail to consider, copy the pocket separately after you make the outer garment pattern. To do this, lay the pocket flat and arrange the outer garment in such a way that the style detail does not obstruct the pocket below. Trace the pocket outline onto the pattern paper.

After you have transferred the pocket outline to a separate pattern piece, remember to mark notches on the side seams to indicate the opening. Add seam allowance to the pattern and label it.

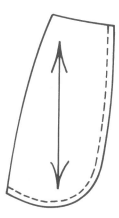

When the pocket is cut as extension of the garment side, it is better to use the original shape as a guide for a new pocket pattern. The pocket can be cut from lightweight fabric, and is sewn to both side and waistline seams for better shape and stability.

SLANT POCKETS

The opening of this inseam pocket extends diagonally, or on a curve, from the waistline to the side seam at the hip. Slant pockets consist of two main pattern pieces, the side pocket piece and the facing. The facing usually is made of lining fabric. The side pocket piece may be cut from the garment fabric if it is not too bulky, or the lower part may be lining fabric, with the visible upper corner section a separate hip panel piece of garment fabric. Sometimes the inner pocket extends across the front and is sewn into a center front zipper seam. A tape stay, cut according to the slant line on the pocket facing pattern, can be sewn into the garment front/facing seam to prevent stretching at this bias edge.

On a tight-fitting garment such as jeans, there may be added ease at the diagonal upper pocket edge to allow room to insert the hand. If such is the case and if the pocket edge is not too bulky, pin a small pleat in the fabric to remove the ease so the hip area will lie flat.

To copy a slant pocket, pin the opening closed across the hip. Pin through the pocket seams to the outside of the garment. Remember to include the seamline of main fabric on the hip panel if lining fabric is used for the inner pocket.

Transfer a parallel grainline from the body onto the pocket area. Copy the pocket directly onto the body of the garment unless the section includes a style detail such as tucks or gathers. To make the pocket pattern, place pattern paper over (if you can see through it) or under the pocket and trace all the pocket lines.

If a style detail is in the way, trace the pocket after the outer garment pattern is made. To do this, lay the pocket flat and arrange the outer garment in such a way that the style detail does not obstruct the pocket below. Transfer the pocket lines to a new piece of pattern paper. Remember to transfer notches for tucks from the outer garment. These will come to your aid when you are checking the pattern and sewing the garment. Add seam allowances at the outer edges.

Make a master pocket pattern.

Make a copy of the pocket pattern shape from the garment pattern. Place pattern paper on top of the lines (if you can see through the paper) or underneath. Transfer the lines to the paper below. This draft will be the master pattern used to make all the other pattern pieces for the pocket, in the order that follows.

ON SOME GARMENTS, THE POCKET
EXTENDS TO CENTER FRONT

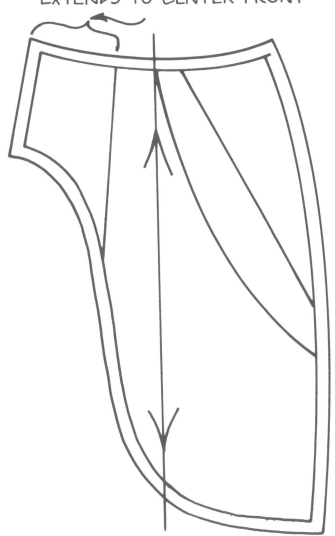

Make the side pocket pattern.

Copy the entire side pocket piece. Transfer
notches where the slanted seam intersects at
the side and waist. Also notch seams where
the hip panel of main fabric will be aligned if
you will use lining fabric for the balance of the
piece. Include notches for tucks, shirring or
any other special details.

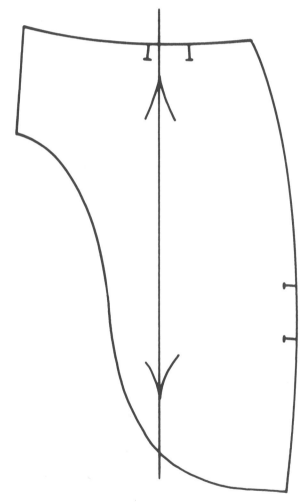

Make a hip panel pattern if necessary.

If you are using lining fabric for the inner pocket pieces—the side pocket and facing—make a separate pattern for a hip overlay. This piece will be cut from garment fabric and stitched on top of the side pocket section at the visible upper corner. Be sure to include notches where the slanted seam of the pocket opening will intersect the waist and side. Add seam allowance at the curved seamline where the piece will be stitched onto the side pocket section.

Make a facing pattern.

Match the facing to the garment body along the diagonal seamline, at the top of the pocket opening at the waistline, and at the side seamline. Match to the back pocket piece around the curved inner edge. Add seam allowance at the diagonal seamline and at the outer edges.

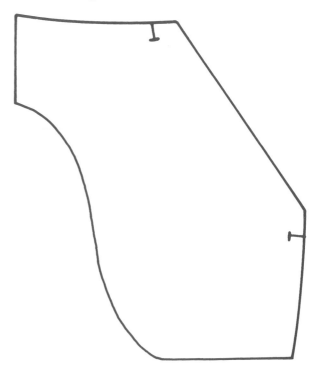

Add back ease that was removed to make the copy.

The diagonal seamline at the upper edge of the pocket facing must match that of the garment body. If you pinched out ease from the upper pocket edge, then you should add it back onto this piece. To do that, cut a line in the paper from the pocket opening to the seamline inside the pocket as shown. Open out the diagonal seam by approximately 1/8 to 1/4 inch (.3 cm to .7 cm) and tape it in place. Blend a smooth seamline.

Match the facing to the garment body at the top of the pocket opening on the waistline as shown. Match the bottom seamline of the pocket to the point where it intersects the side seam of the garment body. Transfer the seamlines from the facing onto the pattern for the garment body. Now the two pieces reflect the necessary ease. Finish the facing pattern as described in the preceding section.

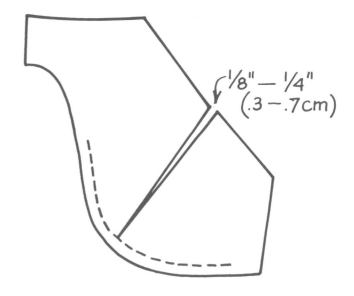

1/8" — 1/4"
(.3 — .7cm)

WELT POCKETS

Welts are fabric strips used to finish a pocket opening that consists of a slash in the body of a garment. The welts can meet at the midpoint of the slash and be of equal size, or one wide welt can cover the entire opening. There will often be a welt pocket on the back of a pair of pants, sometimes with a flap that covers the opening.

It is best that you have some experience sewing these pockets before you attempt to copy them. If you are not familiar with the construction refer to a good sewing book to learn the technique. For that matter, you might use just the pocket from a commercial pattern and transfer it to your garment. You may wish to tape the sewing instructions onto your pattern piece as well.

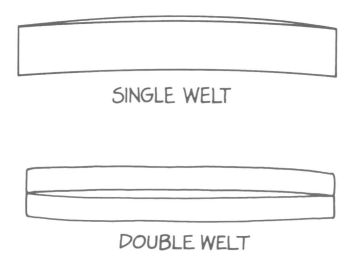

SINGLE WELT

DOUBLE WELT

WAISTBANDS, CUFFS, AND OTHER STRAIGHT PIECES

SOME PATTERN PIECES are best made simply by drafting them. When you copy straight lines in the usual transfer method, they are bound to waver at some point. It is easier to take measurements and draw two parallel straight lines.

First determine the total width of the piece. Measure the finished width, add seam allowance, and double the resulting amount if the piece is on a fold. Draw two parallel lines on the pattern paper, with the space between them the predetermined width of the piece. Then measure the finished length of the piece, and add seam allowances at the ends.

Imagine, for example, that a shirt cuff, with a fold at the lower edge, measures 2 inches (5 cm) wide and 8 inches (20 cm) long. Seam allowances are 1/2 inch (1.5 cm). The pattern piece will be 5 inches (13 cm) wide and 9 inches (23 cm) long.

You can draft a pattern for a waistband with a point on the extension in the same way. Draft a straight band and copy only the extension shape from the garment. When you finish the pattern, walk it to the garment sections to which it will attach. Transfer any necessary notches, such as side seams, pocket placement, and tuck intersections.

On front bands, first transfer the curve at the neckline. Measure down the piece from the neckline to determine the finished length. Add seam allowances. You may also wish to mark for buttonhole and button placement.

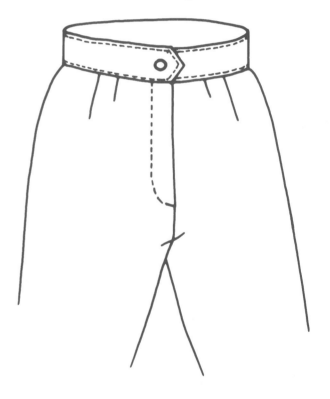

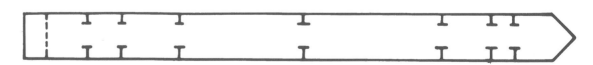

FACINGS

PATTERN PIECES FOR FACINGS can easily be drafted from the garment pattern itself. Facings attach to the outer edge of the garment and fold back to the inside. Front facings also can be extensions of the garment front edge, folded to the inside.

If the facing is even in width, measure the depth of the facing, plus the seam allowance if it is needed. Then simply trace the outer edge of the original pattern and measure in from the edge to make the cutting line for the facing.

If the facing is uneven in width, transfer the shape to the outside of the garment. To do this, pin through all layers of fabric from the inside along the edge of the facing so that the pins are visible from the outside. When you make the pattern for the body of the garment, include this line as well. To make the facing pattern, place pattern paper over (if you can see through the paper) or under the body pattern, and transfer the facing outline. Add seam allowances to the inner facing edge if needed.

Facings are one area in which it is a simple matter to improve upon the quality of the original garment when you make your copy. In ready-to-wear garments, facings are often rather skimpy. It takes just a few extra minutes to widen a facing and create a more luxurious garment.

A too-narrow back neck facing, for instance, has the aggravating habit of creeping to the outside whenever you wear the garment. If you make the facing deeper at the center back, it will stay inside the garment where it belongs.

To make this change, first copy the original facing. Then measure down to the desired new depth at center back (5 inches, or 12 cm, is very generous) and blend a new line to meet the old at the shoulder seam.

Facings can also contribute style details to the garment. You might topstitch them in place on the outside of the garment—a small step that will make a big change in the garment's appearance.

On the blouse shown in the photograph, facings are used decoratively in another way. Two separate facings, one wider than the other, are turned to the outside at the neckline. The outer edges are turned under and edgestitched in place.

Make the facing patterns from the front and back bodice patterns. For the blouse shown, both front and back facings are layered. Both layers are cut to the neckline edge. The outer edge of the narrower facing was turned under and stitched to the wider facing. The front and back sections were joined at the shoulders, then stitched to the garment neckline. Then the outer edge of the piece was turned under and edgestitched on the outside of the garment.

The concept is a simple one, but imagine the possibilities. The facings could be made of a contrasting color. You might also use scraps of a print fabric, left from a skirt, to trim a solid-color blouse.

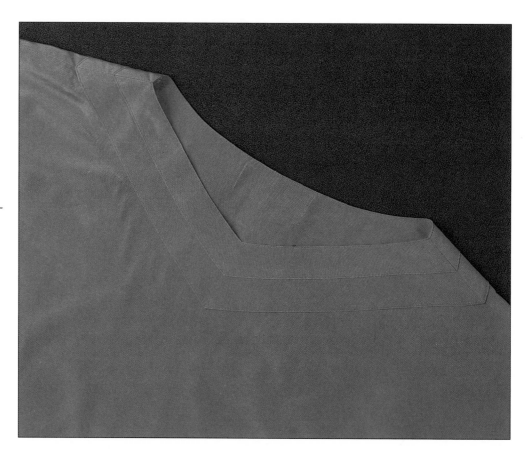

LINING PATTERNS CAN easily be made
from the garment pattern pieces. Some
garments are lined to the outer edges,
in which case you can cut lining from the
garment pattern itself.. Make a notation on
the pattern to cut both outer fabric and lining.

On a lined garment which also has facings,
the lining usually is sewn to the inner facing
edges. To copy this lining, begin by outlining
the facings as described on page 95. Copy the
facing lines onto the garment body pattern.
Make a copy of this pattern, and cut it along
the facing lines. The inner section of the
pattern piece can be used to make the lining
pattern and the outer section can be used
for the facings. Add seam allowances and
notches where facing and lining pieces
will be sewn together.

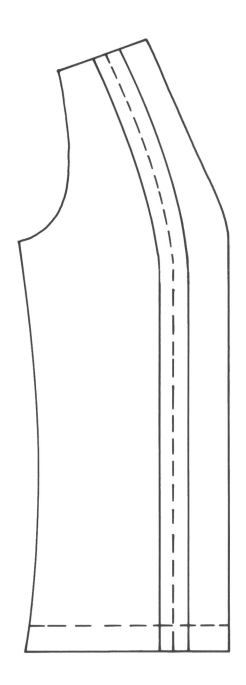

Sometimes the back lining has a center pleat. If this is the case with your garment, begin by measuring the depth of the pleat. Copy the garment back pattern and add the depth of the pleat at center back. Notch the top and bottom at the original center back. The pleat will automatically be doubled because the back is either on a fold or will be cut as two pieces.

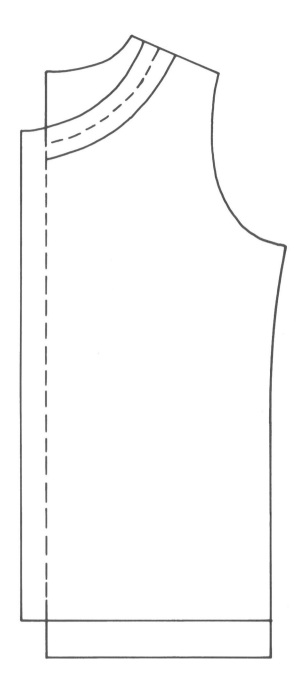

YOU WILL NEED a plywood surface in order to copy a garment that has elastic at the waist, cuffs, etc. The elastic must be stretched so that the garment fabric is smooth and flat. Ordinary straight pins won't hold securely enough; it is best to use push pins to secure the elasticized section, and actually hammer them into place if necessary.

Stretch the piece only until the garment lies flat. With knits, especially, take care not to overstretch. An alternative is to open up the casing and release the elastic to make the copy.

If the elastic casing is a fabric extension folded to the inside, as is often found at the waistline of pants, the seam allowances should be shaped on the casing extension. On the pattern, fold the extension to the inside just as if it were being sewn, when you cut out the pattern piece.

Use a measuring tape to measure the elastic itself, inching your way around the garment while the elastic is in a relaxed state. The measurements will need some adjustment since elastics vary greatly in their degree of stretch. This is especially true of elastics stitched with commercial multineedle equipment, often found on waistbands. If the garment you are copying was constructed this way, try a stitch-through elastic for your copy. Elastic shirring is done commercially with multineedle machinery that allows for regulation of the tension on the elasticized thread. This effect cannot be duplicated with a home sewing machine. You might consider using a wide stitch-through elastic instead, or the type with an encased drawcord. Whatever you choose to do, figure it out before you make your copy. You may need to make a separate casing or adjust your pattern in some other way.

SHOULDER PADS

SHOULDER PADS in unlined garments should be covered. The garment fabric can be used if it is not too stiff or bulky, or a coordinating lining fabric can be substituted. Here is a helpful tip for covering a triangular-shaped shoulder pad: Cut the fabric on the bias. The fabric will roll smoothly over the wider upper surface of the pad. Manufacturers may use shoulder pad shapes that you cannot buy, so check for availability before you make a pattern for the covering.

Remember always to remove the shoulder pad from the side of the garment you copy. Left in place, it can result in an inaccurate pattern piece.

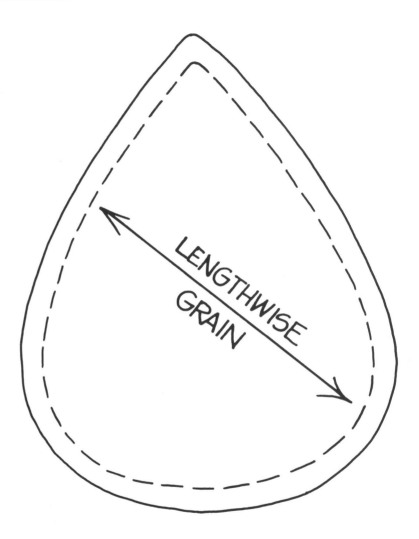

LENGTHWISE GRAIN

A GARMENT ON WHICH the style lines differ on the left and right sides is copied in a slightly different way. The procedure is the same, except that you use the center of the garment as an alignment point. Copy one side of the garment, then turn it over and realign the second side on the center line, making sure the upper and lower edges are even with those of the first half of the pattern. Then copy the second half.

Mark all pattern pieces "right side up" to remind yourself that the pattern and the fabric should be face up for cutting. If this step is overlooked, the style lines could be reversed.

The blouse shown in the photograph has a placket at the left shoulder, which means that both front and back pattern pieces are dissimilar on the right and left sides. On this particular blouse, however, the left and right sides of the bodice pieces need not be copied separately.

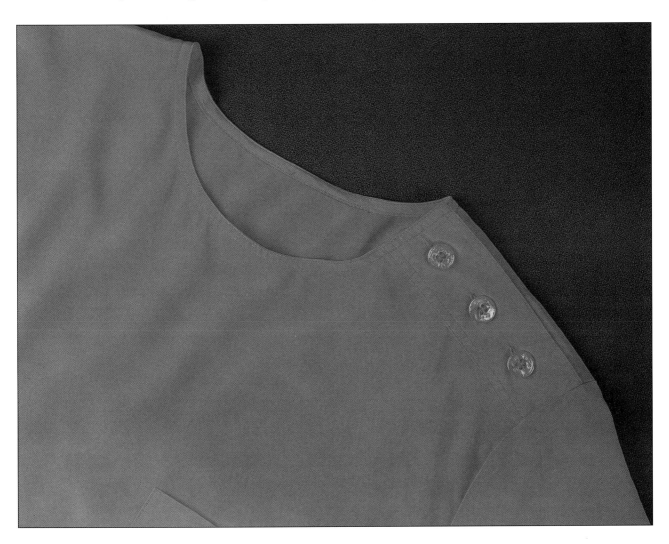

For the front pattern, use a piece of paper wide enough to copy the entire front rather than just one side, and draw a lengthwise line at the center of the piece. Locate the center front lengthwise grainline on the blouse. Secure the left side, with the pocket and shoulder detail, for copying. Transfer in the usual way. Transfer the placket seamline below the shoulder buttons as well.

Add seam allowances to the pattern all the way around. To ensure that the halves of the pattern are identical, do this: Fold the pattern in half along the center line. Cut it out roughly, leaving an inch (2.5 cm) or so around the outer edges. Staple the halves together, working in a zigzag line, with one staple in the seam allowance, the next just outside the outer edge, the next in the seam allowance, and so on around the piece. Cut out the pattern piece then remove the staples.

For the left shoulder, tape on a piece of paper at the shoulder stitching line. Fold the extension down from that stitching line onto the front of the pattern. Measure down and draw a line to represent the width of the placket with seam allowance added. Fold under the seam allowance as it will be stitched. With the placket folded in place, cut along the neckline and armhole to create a shaped seam allowance.

Copy the back bodice in the same way. On the left shoulder, the back extends under the front by the width of the placket, with a self facing that folds back and is stitched down at the shoulder line.

Make the pattern for the entire back and tape a piece of paper at the left shoulder stitching line as before. This time continue the shoulder onto the front. Measure the width of the placket. Measure out from the stitching line on the shoulder by the width of the placket and draw a line. Then repeat this step since the extension folds back, and add seam allowance at the shoulder.

Fold the pattern back at the extension/facing foldline and fold under the seam allowance as it will be stitched on the shoulder line. Match the back pattern to the front at the shoulder and transfer the neckline and armhole shaping. Since the front will overlap the back, the seamlines must correspond. Then cut to create a shaped seam allowance.

Remember to label the pattern pieces "right side up."

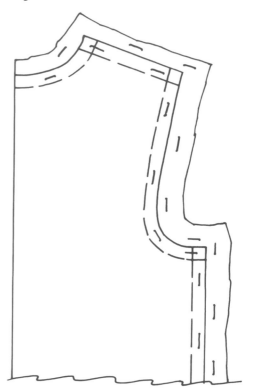

KNITS ARE COPIED the same way as all other garments. Make sure, though, not to stretch the garment out of shape when securing it. A small error can make a big difference. If the pattern is cut just 1/8 inch (.3 cm) wider at each side seam, the finished garment will be 1/2 inch (1.2 cm) bigger around. For that reason, it may be worthwhile to measure across the garment while it is in a relaxed state and compare to your pattern for accuracy.

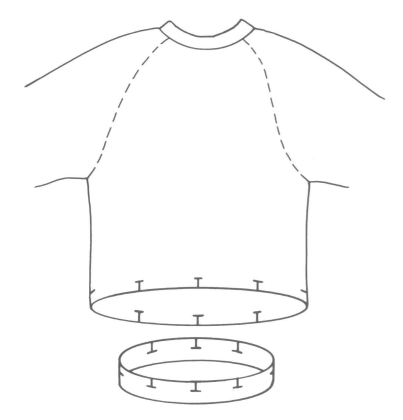

Knits will vary in their degree of stretch. It is important to make your copy in a fabric with the same stretch factor. With ribbed knits such as those used in waistbands, neckbands, and cuffs, the pattern will otherwise have to be adjusted to accommodate the stretch factor of your replacement fabric.

RIBBED NECKBANDS, COLLARS AND CUFFS

Patterns for ribbed knit bands can usually be drafted from measurements These pieces often are straight bands of fabric. Measure the length and width of the piece and add seam allowances. Take care not to stretch the ribbing while taking the measurements.

Notches are very important in helping you achieve an even amount of stretch around a banded piece. A banded waist, for example, may have only one seam. This seam is usually aligned with the side or center back seam of the garment. Place notches on the waistband to correspond with the side seams and center front and back. The band will be stretched between these points when sewn. If necessary, the piece can be further divided into eighths with notches. Placing the notches closer together may help keep the piece more manageable.

USING YOUR PATTERN CREATIVELY

NOW THAT YOU are confident you can copy virtually any garment, your potential as a designer is practically limitless. Your existing wardrobe can be transformed to reflect all the latest style changes.

Go shopping, look at magazines, and copy whatever appeals to you. Set up a file system to organize design ideas you find in magazines and mail-order catalogues, or sketches of garments that strike your fancy. Label a large envelope for each garment category—dresses, pants, blouses, skirts, coats, and so on—then file your clippings and sketches for future reference. When you plan a new blouse, for example, you can check the file to refresh yourself as to blouse details you especially liked, then incorporate them into your new garment design.

When you have a pattern that fits well, updating it with new design details is a simple matter. Perhaps you have made a jacket that fits perfectly, but after a few years its style is a bit outdated. First you need to identify the problem. It may be too long for today's look, or the lapels might be too wide.

Try on the current jacket style, make a few notes, and take measurements if possible. Then adjust your old pattern to reflect the changes. A jacket lapel can be narrowed easily: Just draw in a new seamline along the collar edge. Take care to make the same changes on the facing pattern.

Even small details can make a big difference. Contrast piping sewn along a yoke seam can give an otherwise simple blouse a whole new look. Consider also replacing the buttons with new ones in the contrast color to complete the transformation.

Combining different prints or fabrics on a garment can also give new life to an old pattern. Splicing together dissimilar fabrics, however, can be tricky. Take care to preshrink all the fabrics. Make sure the dyes are colorfast and will not bleed or crock onto an adjoining part of the garment.

Suppose you have a good, simple pattern and would like to change the style by adding a few seamlines for interest. To change a style line, make a copy of your pattern and draw in the new lines where you want them. Cut the pattern apart along the new lines and add seam allowance to both pieces. Add a few notches, too, to help you piece the sections accurately.

For another simple change to a plain button-front shirt pattern, attach a hidden front placket. Add a little decorative stitching down the front and you have created a unique variation for your basic shirt pattern.

Have fun expressing yourself through the clothes you make. Take pride in your finished work. Experiment with your patterns and make your clothes a reflection of you.

A SAMPLING OF GARMENTS

THE GARMENTS SHOWN on the following pages were chosen to illustrate unusual design features or complicated construction details that require a slightly different copying approach. It is interesting design, in addition to good fit, that makes a garment worth repeating.

Today's clothing styles tend toward simpler lines and unstructured shapes. This is an advantage to manufacturers, since a smaller range of sizes is needed to fit a larger portion of the population. Older garments such as these exhibit a wealth of interesting design details and imaginative ways of adapting clothing to fit the human shape.

These garments were discovered in consignment shops and other used clothing outlets. Many show signs of hard wear. They are definitely not stylish—a few of them are downright unappealing—but each has at least one unique element that is worth noting and that offers a lesson to be learned. You most likely won't wish to duplicate one of these garments, but you may find a special detail to incorporate into a garment of your own.

Many of these garments exhibit careful coordination of fabric and design. Some of the design details would not have worked at all well if the garment had been made of fabric with very different characteristics. In any copying project, it is a good idea to use fabric with similar qualities to those of the original garment, or to test the pattern in a fabric similar to the one you plan to use.

BLACK SEQUINED JACKET

The fitted black evening jacket is unlined and is made of moderately lightweight rayon crepe that allows the shirring at the lower front to drape nicely. On each side of the front, the shirred section extends from a vertical slash on the lower edge to the side seam.

The right front would be used to make the copy because it is the side to which the button loops are sewn. To copy the front, first secure the right front edge to the grainline marked on the paper. Secure the neckline and shoulder up to the first seam on the shoulder dart and transfer to the paper below. Shift the top of the dart over, following the procedure for copying darts. When you fold the dart for a shaped seam allowance, note that the folds in this case are pressed toward the armhole, not toward the center of the garment.

The rest of the front can be copied down to the beginning of the gathered section on the side seam. Transfer from the front along the waistline and up the seam where the gathered section is attached.

The easiest way to copy the gathered section is by measuring it with a tape, holding the tape about an inch away from the seam and measuring from the upper edge of the section to the lower edge. Once you have that measurement, you can draft this section to complete the front. Remember to measure along the hem as well, since the section is wider at the hem than at the upper edge. The drawing shows the shape of the finished pattern piece.

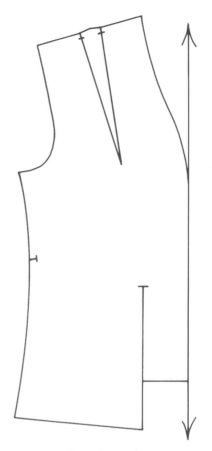

The narrow jacket sleeve has an unusual finishing touch. The lower end of the underarm seam was left open for approximately 2 inches (5 cm). A one-piece facing is sewn to both seam allowances, providing a seam into which the button loops were sewn.

If you wish to copy the exact placement of the sequins, or similar decorative additions to any garment, it is easy to make a template for the purpose. Place a piece of pattern paper or tracing paper over the design area and make a rubbing with a soft-leaded pencil or a piece of colored chalk. Trace the lines onto the garment pieces after the shoulder darts are sewn. If the template is made from the right side of the garment, remember to turn it face down when you transfer the pattern to the left side.

DOUBLE-BREASTED BLOUSE

The styling details on this vest-front blouse are well worth noticing even though the workmanship and fabric quality are only fair.

The double button closure on the front could be applied to almost any blouse. Simply extend the front edge by another inch (2.5 cm) or so beyond the center front line to allow for the additional row of buttons. Widen the facing by the same amount.

One of the most intriguing aspects of the blouse is a shirred area below the non-functional pocket welt that creates the effect of a small peplum. The visible seamline extending from the end of the welt and the side seam is a clue to the construction. The remainder of the seam is covered by the welt.

The pattern for the blouse front involved a slash cut across the lower bodice, with the lower section extending a few inches beyond the side seam to allow for the shirring.

The entire front can be secured and copied in the standard way across to the beginning of the gathered section. That area must be isolated and copied after the other seamlines have been transferred.

The technique used in copying the gathered area is similar to that used for other shirred areas, described on page 72. Follow the garment hemline, laying it flat and marking approximately 1 inch (2.5 cm) of the gathered seamline, then shift to transfer the next short section. When the entire seamline has been transferred to the paper, link the dots to create a smooth line. Mark in the seamline directly above the newly shifted area. Then link the dots to create a smooth seamline.

The lower ends of the sleeves are finished in the simplest possible way. The seam was left open for approximately 1-1/2 inches (4 cm) above the cuff seamline to allow an overlap for the button closure. The seam was pressed open and the seam allowance edges finished with a serger.

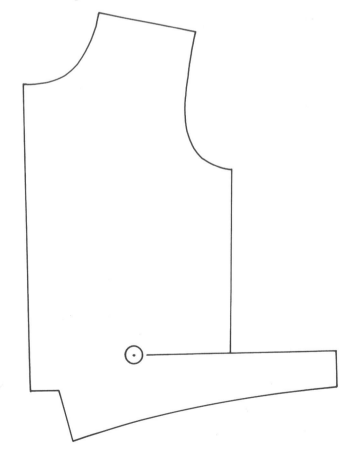

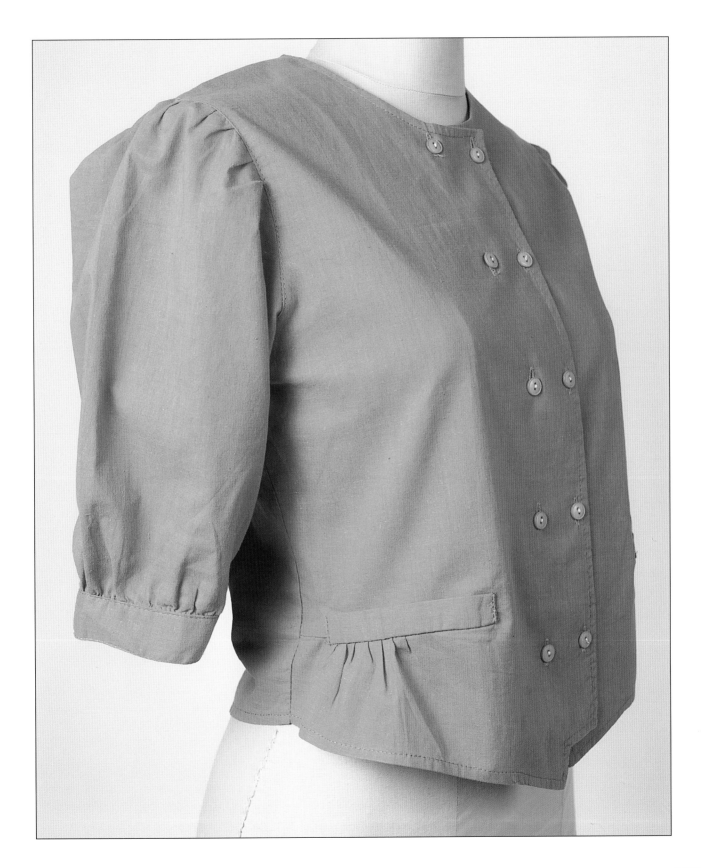

SCALLOP-EDGED SHIRT

The design of this shirt is straightforward and absolutely traditional up to the scalloped facing seamline along the right front edge. The scallop pattern stops at the waistline; the edge of the garment below the waist is straight so that there is no irregular line to show through the pants or skirt.

A manufactured garment is not necessarily perfect, as you well know. A design that requires careful stitching as this one does can often be better executed by a home sewer who is not rushing to meet a quota.

The shirt can be copied in the standard manner. It would be better, however to draft a new pattern for the front seamline detail. An expanding metal sewing gauge could be used to space the scallops evenly. Then a template could be made for the single scallop pattern. The template could also be used to chalk in the stitching line on the garment piece to ensure accurate sewing.

This design, or some variation of it, could be adapted to almost any shirt pattern. It is a simple alteration, and the resulting garment will bear little resemblance to an often-used basic pattern.

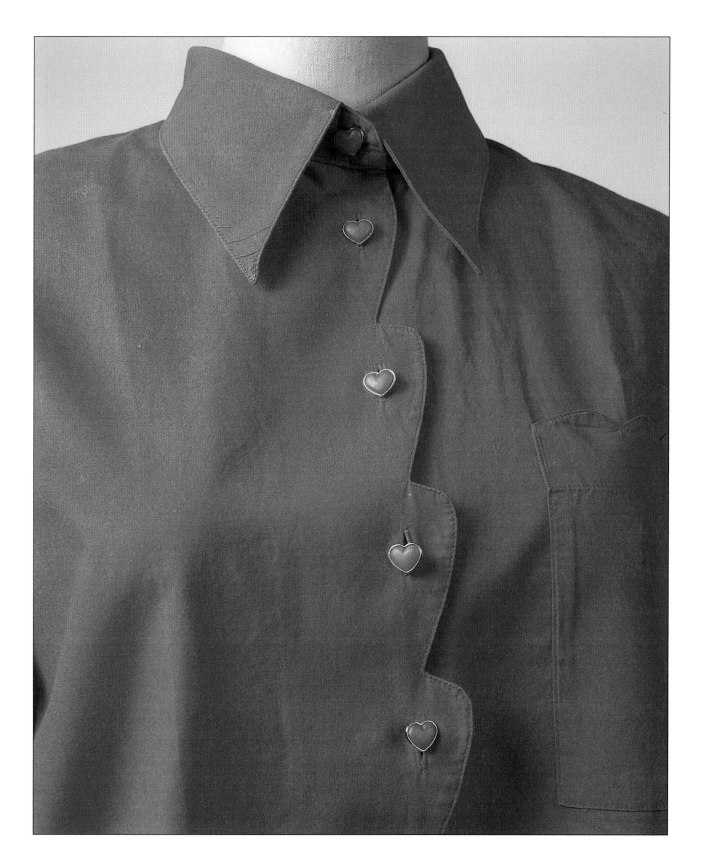

BLOUSE WITH JEWELED TAB

The most eye-catching aspect of this blouse is the beaded decoration at the neckline. The beading was worked on a separate shaped tab that can be removed before the blouse is laundered or dry cleaned. The upper edge of the tab follows the contour of the collar seamline. The tab buttons invisibly in place under the collar points.

The front button closure is completely hidden within two pleated panels down the front of the blouse. This is an unusual treatment that could work with any blouse that buttons down the front.

To copy the front of the blouse, it would be easiest to pleat the pattern paper first, following the procedure described on page 69. The remainder of the front could be copied in the usual way, with the shirred seams copied according to the instructions on page 73.

The blouse has no shoulder seams. Instead, the back extends well to the front over the shoulders, creating the impression of a front yoke. The front of the blouse is wider at the shoulder seamline and is gathered to fit the back piece at the seamlines.

The whole back piece could not be laid flat for copying, so a realignment point would have to be established at the shoulder. The procedure for copying the back of this blouse would be similar to that used to copy a dolman sleeve, described on page 80.

COLOR WAVES

This dress is fun! It inspires all sorts of ideas for variations on the same theme. Copy any basic pattern you own, a T-shirt for instance, and draw in any style lines you like—straight, curved, or whatever. Then cut along the new lines and add seam allowance at the cut edges. Piecing fabrics this way is easy to do.

To ensure good results when you piece a garment, it is best to use assorted colors of the same fabric, or fabrics that are very much alike. If you are determined to use dissimilar fabrics together, experiment first with scraps to make sure the fabrics are compatible.

This dress was made in a firm wool double knit, which is the key to its success. The thickness and stability of the fabric helps the garment keep its shape.

In construction, all of the seams were clipped and pressed open. The curves would not be smooth and flat if the seam allowances all had been pressed to one side or the other.

The procedure for copying any garment with an asymmetrical style line is as follows:

Use a piece of pattern paper wide enough for the entire front or back of the garment and draw the lengthwise grainline toward the center. Only half the garment need be copied for the structural seams, but a complete front and back will be needed for the design seams.

Copy the structural seams in the usual way. Transfer the design seams on half of the garment you have used. Fold the pattern at the center line and trace the structural seamlines to the second half. Then turn the garment to the other side and realign the center on the grainline, matching seamlines to the pattern lines at the neckline and hem. Transfer the design seamlines on this side, making sure they meet the previously transferred lines at center front and center back.

When the front or back pattern piece is finished, cut it apart along the design seamlines. Trace the pieces onto a new sheet of paper, and add seam allowance at each cut edge to complete the pattern.

THE GARDENING PANTS

It is obvious that these well-worn pants are their owner's favorite. The irregular design lines contribute to the garment's comfortable fit as well as to its appearance.

The front leg consists of three separate panels. One includes the inseam and the crotch area. On it is a center seam that ends inside an inverted box pleat at the waistline. The pleat is stitched closed from the waist to the lower end of the belt loop.

The outer side of the front leg is a separate piece with an extension to the side seam for the pocket opening. The pocket extension has a self facing and is sewn to the inner pocket section.

The pocket has a stay extension that is sewn into the front zipper seam. A pocket stay helps maintain the lines of the garment front and prevents the pleats from being pulled out of shape.

This pocket would best be copied separately from the outer garment. To do that, turn the leg inside out and secure and transfer the pocket outline in the usual manner.

The third front leg piece is a very narrow strip at the side seamline. The pocket opening extension overlaps it in the hip area.

The back of the leg is a single piece and can be copied in the standard way.

These pants are made of sturdy cotton twill fabric, which has fine diagonal ridges on the face side. It is easiest to identify the grainline by looking at the wrong side of the fabric. The crossgrain is readily apparent and the lengthwise grain can be marked by chalking a line at a right angle to the crossgrain.

CIRCULAR RUFFLES

Every now and then circular ruffles reappear as important fashion details. Such a ruffle is usually found at the neckline, although sometimes it may take the form of a jabot on the front of a blouse. Perhaps you've seen a circular ruffle at the end of a sleeve or on a skirt hem.

When copying a circular ruffle—or any circularly cut piece—it is most important to identify the grainline correctly. The beautiful soft drape achieved by the bias cut will be lost if the grainline is not correct.

It may not always be possible to copy a circular ruffle as one piece. In this case, pin or chalk a line on the ruffle to divide it for copying. Draw a line on the pattern paper to represent that division. Secure the ruffle to the division line. On one side of the division line smooth and secure the ruffle to make the copy.

After the first section has been transferred, release all of the pins except at the division line and start there to realign the other half of the ruffle. With the rest of the garment freed up you can smooth and secure the second half of the ruffle to finish the copy.

The ruffle at the neckline of this blouse ends at the shoulder. It is not quite a circle; the shape of the pattern piece is shown in the drawing.

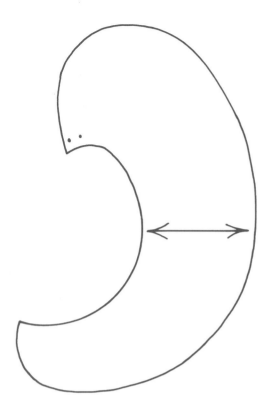

DRESS WITH BACK DETAIL

The addition of a modified circular ruffle at the lower back of this dress provides an elegant style detail. The straight silhouette of the dress is undisturbed, yet the ruffle adds softness to the lines.

Vertical seams were added from the shoulders to the hem. The ruffle is attached at the curved lower edge of the central panel.

The garment could be copied in the usual manner. The lower back inset should be copied as if it were a circular ruffle; the procedure is explained on page 118. With this inset, as with any bias-cut piece, it is very important to follow the grainlines of the original garment.

The front of the dress has very simple lines. It has a low V neckline and an edgestitched band 1-1/4 inches (3 cm) wide attached along each front edge to the shoulder seamline. It buttons to just above the knee.

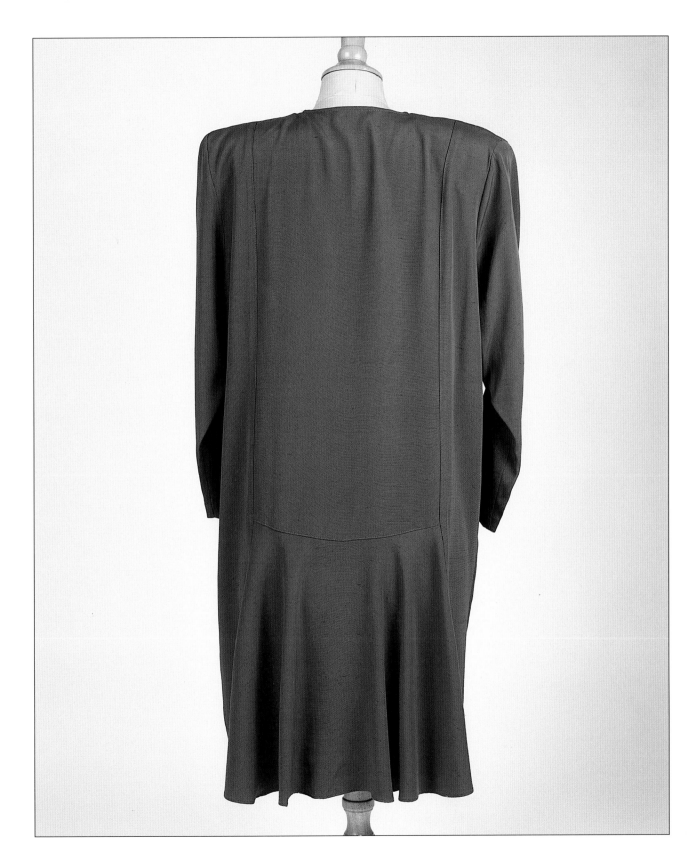

HOODED TOP

Hoods reappear on the fashion scene every several years, usually on sportswear. The hood on this blouse is strictly ornamental, although on a copy made in slightly heavier fabric it could function perfectly well.

The hood has a center seam. The entire half could be secured so that it could be copied in one piece. It is important not to distort a bias-cut seam, like the one at this neckline, when making a copy.

A hood could replace a traditional collar on almost any shirt or blouse. Just find one to

copy, then alter the neckline of the blouse to match that of the hood.

Another noteworthy detail on the blouse is the "darts." They are actually tucks. They are not sewn to points at the upper ends, but are sewn part way then release as would any tucks. They could be copied as if they were shaped darts, according to the instructions on page 60. Any dart can be changed to a tuck: Simply end the stitching before reaching the point.

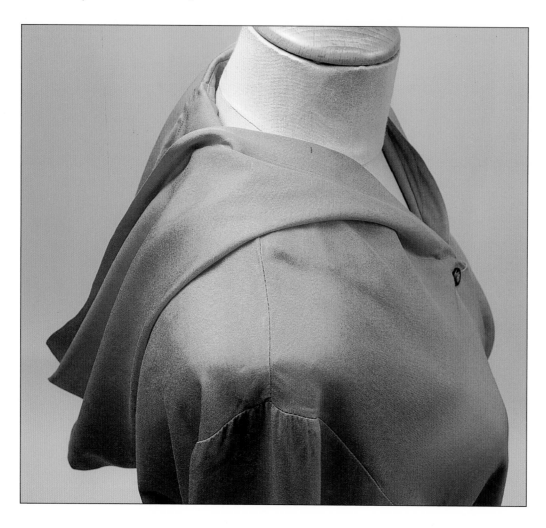

SKIRT WITH A YOKE

Many garment styles include a V-shaped seamline at the front, with an attached gathered skirt. The same style line is a traditional feature on the front of a wedding dress.

The front and the back of this skirt yoke are divided into quarters; the additional seams allow the garment to be shaped around the hips. The yoke can be copied in the usual manner.

To make the skirt pattern, secure the skirt at the center front grainline. Pin the side seamline from the hem up to the point beyond which the garment will no longer lie flat.

Place a row of pins across the skirt to isolate the gathered area. Transfer the hem and side seam up to the isolated area. Remove all the pins except the row that isolates the gathered section.

Starting at the center front, mark in the ditch of the gathered seam directly above the row of pins. Inching your way across the seam a little at a time, continue transferring to the paper. As you proceed, remove pins from the previously transferred section to free up the garment so it can be shifted further. Continue this way across to the side seam. Blend the marks on the pattern to create a smooth seamline.

The lower skirt pattern will not look much like the garment itself. The diagonal upper edge will slope much more gradually toward the center point. After all the fabric has been gathered up to fit the shorter yoke edge, the shape will be more pronounced.

PARTY DRESS

Judging from the condition of this colorful dress, it danced till dawn on more than one occasion before being relegated to the consignment shop! The prominent feature is the unusual cut of the skirt. A single piece extends from the back seam to each side of the center front panel—there are no side seams.

This would be a very difficult garment to copy because of the many tucks along the front panel seam and because the side sections are on the bias.

Just this once, it would be best to let out seams to make the copy. It would be nearly impossible to make an accurate copy with the garment intact. If the front panel seam were opened along one long edge, and the waistline seam opened from the panel to the bodice side seam, the center back seam could be secured and the rest of the skirt laid flat for copying. Because of the bias cut, care would have to be taken to avoid distorting the piece during the copying process.

There will be rare occasions when it is simply easiest to let out a seam in order to make a good pattern. Look at it this way: You are planning to sew an entire garment—repairing just one seam is a very small task by comparison.

A Vintage Dress

Heirloom garments such as this unique dress often have unusual styling that is rarely seen on today's clothes. If you make a study of vintage clothing, you may find a number of ideas that can be incorporated into your own designs. It is quite possible that even the professional designers take inspiration from such sources. Fashion does repeat itself, with only minor variations each time around.

The dress fabric is extraordinary. There is a lot of texture to it, with its raised clipped yarns creating a checkerboard pattern in one area and a stripe in another. The grainline has been reversed on some sections of the garment to add interest. The effect can be seen on the sleeves, at the neckline, and on the center back panel.

The strip of fur visible at the hemline is actually attached to the lower edge of an overskirt, providing more texture still. Narrow piping defines the seamline where the skirt meets the bodice.

Although this dress probably doesn't resemble any garment you would wish to duplicate, copying it would present no problems. The pattern of the fabric identifies the grainlines, and the lines of the dress itself are reasonably straight.

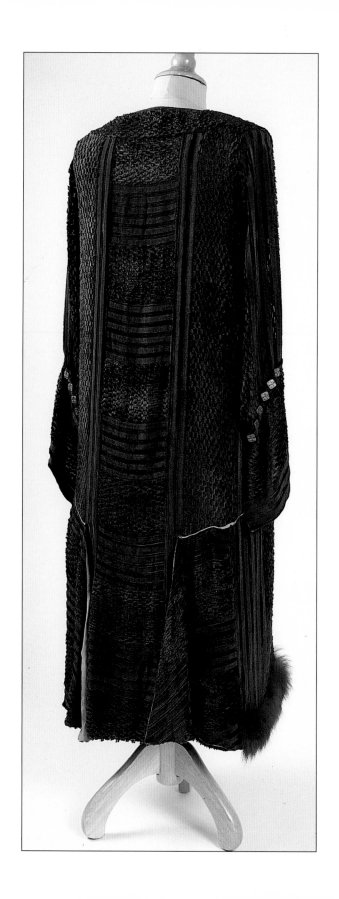

INDEX

Our gratitude to the people at G Street Fabrics, Rockville, Maryland, who supplied us with the needle-point tracing wheels used to demonstrate the copying process for the photographs in this book.